BEYOND TH

Dear Ron,

I am delighted that I was able to start you on your Masonic Journey.

It can be as long as you want it to be.

Yours with best wishes affectionately

P. Ronson.

BEYOND THE CRAFT

Keith B. Jackson

First published 1980
Fourth edition 1994
Reprinted 1998
This impression 2002

ISBN 0 85318 207 8

All rights reserved. No part of this book may be
reproduced or transmitted in any form or by any means,
electronic or mechanical, including photocopying,
recording or by any information storage and retrieval
system, without permission from the Publisher in writing.

© K. B. Jackson 1980

Published by Lewis Masonic

an imprint of Ian Allan Publishing Ltd,
Hersham, Surrey KT12 4RG.
Printed by Ian Allan Printing Ltd,
Hersham, Surrey KT12 4RG.

Contents

Publishers note to the Fourth Edition

In a little over one year, the first edition of *Beyond the Craft* sold out. This book has now become a standard source of reference to many as a means of introduction to masonic degrees and orders 'beyond the craft'. The demand and interest shewn amongst brethren worldwide has indicated that the need for such a volume has been long overdue.

With this fourth edition we have taken the opportunity to revise certain of the chapters by correcting a few historical inaccuracies and changes in regalia requirements that had been made since the first edition was published. The illustrations have now been reproduced in colour to enhance the book further.

We believe that this book will continue to provide a valuable introduction to the various degrees and orders for many years to come.

September 1994

Foreword

It is both an honour and a pleasure to be asked to contribute a word or two to Keith Jackson's book, and to recommend it to the Craft—which I do right heartily. I have known Bro Jackson for many years and am aware of the zeal with which he has, through his splendidly illustrated talks, aroused interest and enthusiasm among the brethren for exploration of the ultra-Craft degrees and Orders. I suspect that not a few of those who have figured in the recent steady expansion in their membership (certainly in the West Country) owe their increase in masonic knowledge to Bro Jackson's persuasive revelations. He has rightly drawn aside veils which, for many years, have clothed some of the more recondite degrees with unfathomable and unnecessary mystique.

Bro Alvin Langdon Coburn's entirely apposite title, *Beyond the Craft*, commended itself to me at the time when I was myself under the influence of that eminent masonic student and writer, and I have consistently used it, and in particular for my own paper on the subject. Bro Langdon Coburn, in fact, himself conferred one of the degrees upon me at Llandudno and then led me into another at Manchester, where I met for the first time Bro Fred Pick whose admirable work in the two 'Pick and Knight' books has been entrusted to me to preserve and revise. It will not be generally known that Langdon Coburn, as well as being a profoundly perceptive freemason who loved the additional degrees, enjoyed, in the early part of the century, worldwide renown as a photographic artist. His work in this field is still greatly honoured. He was, incidentally, of American birth but had long made his home in the U.K. His own paper, *Beyond the Craft* (*The*

Freemasons' Magazine, No. 664, 1950), has never been bettered.

Bro Jackson has placed the Craft in his debt by making available in a much expanded form the information which he has for long been disseminating through his talks to lodges and study societies. Some of the details now given to us have never before been in print in any form, and I for one have learned a great deal. There is much in these pages to interest and enlighten and I trust that many more brethren may be encouraged, 'without detriment to themselves or their connections', to broaden their masonic experience and, through their membership in some of the wonderful and colourful branches of the freemasonic structure, find that there is much more in pure antient Craft Masonry than they had previously comprehended.

Frederick Smyth
Master (1979–80)
Quatuor Coronati Lodge No. 2076

Introduction

I am sure that many masonic readers have overheard those engrossing snippets of conversation that seem to occur so frequently at the festive board of a Craft lodge where reference is made to 'the Mariners', 'the KT' or 'the Cryptic'. Enquiry is rewarded with the explanation that they are other degrees, but generally there is little further information forthcoming and one is left with a feeling of awakened, yet ungratified curiosity.

Many of us I am sure have made effort to satisfy this curiosity by reference to any masonic volume that might be available but, alas, in most instances one is unsuccessful, except perhaps for a generalised section within a book that gives the briefest of all detail, again leaving this quest for knowledge unfulfilled. This information, however, is to be found, but unfortunately it is spread piecemeal throughout many, many volumes, most of which are not readily available to the majority of freemasons. Feeling that this situation indicates a definite need on the part of the zealous and enquiring brother, I have attempted to produce a condensed, yet comprehensive text of information regarding the various masonic Orders at work in England today.

It is well to remember that masonic degrees are a vital means of teaching lessons in the value of such virtues as Honesty, Charity, Industry, Fidelity, Humility and such like, and for the most part they have been developed into Orders which have been superimposed on the basis of the Craft degrees and therefore it is not surprising that in many cases, the common starting point is the ordinary masonic qualification of Master Mason. In some cases there is a further link with the Craft in as much that the rulers are required to have passed through the chair of a Craft lodge.

A very eminent brother by the name of Alvin Langdon Coburn, who was prominent in most degrees of freemasonry during his lifetime; coined the phrase 'beyond the Craft', when engaged in his various masonic writings; and as it so aptly describes the regions we are about to explore, I adopted it as what I considered to be a fitting title for this book. The degrees beyond the Craft are known by various titles, but none can be fairly said to offer an accurate description. The terms generally used are 'side degrees', 'advanced' and even 'higher degrees', the latter two usually stimulating strong protest and resentment from the many avid supporters of the Craft. This is understandable for that which can produce the oldest authentic records must naturally be in that regard the senior and highest, and this of course is the Craft. It appears that the most reasonable title would be to describe them as additional degrees, for this is exactly what they are.

Their history is even more obscure and chequered than the Craft, for in early days many of these degrees were conferred in a somewhat haphazard manner; it was quite normal for two or three brethren to take a candidate aside following an ordinary lodge meeting, and entrust him with the grip, token and words in a very simple ceremony. There are, however, certain degrees which could never have been transmitted in this fashion as the ritual and symbolism was much more elaborate, demanding the facilities of a temple in its entirety; and in addition there are others, which it is claimed by certain writers, to have been developed by 18th-century operative masons, to distinguish themselves from these innovators—'the speculatives'.

Be that as it may, it is first necessary to quickly glimpse at the development of masonry generally to even begin to contemplate the evolution of the many other degrees. The first Grand Lodge of England came into being in 1717 and became known as 'the Moderns', a term of derision employed by the opposing Grand Lodge of 'Antients' (formed in 1751); and while the premier Grand Lodge frowned on all activities beyond the three recognised degrees of the Craft, the Antients basically allowed their lodges to practise any and all degrees under the authority of their Craft Warrant. Eventually these two Grand Lodges were to join forces, when in 1813 they became the United Grand Lodge of Antient Free and Accepted Masons of England, and in their Articles of Union was included under Article II. 'It is declared and pronounced that pure Antient Masonry consists of three degrees, and no more, viz, those of the Entered Apprentice, the Fellow Craft, and the Master Mason, including the Supreme Order of the Holy Royal Arch.'

By the time of the Union a considerable amount of revision had taken place in the ritual, with the alteration of a certain Clause within the Constitution, which changed the basis of masonry from being Christian to that of Non-Christian. Also the period 1740–1800 saw the rise of a host of so-called masonic Rites and degrees on the European Continent, that were fabricated by those to whom our operative tradition was not sufficient, and who devised ceremonies which enlarged and expanded the scope of the recognised masonic domain to encompass all manner of elaboration. On the other hand, an examination of some rituals in use today within 'other Orders', can be seen to demonstrate features that were once part of early Craft or Royal Arch working. A distinctive example is the ceremony of *Passing the Veils*, once part of the English Royal Arch ritual and now only to be found in Bristol and Irish Chapters. It is still preserved, however, in Scotland and in some Commonwealth countries as the separate degree of Excellent Master. Of the degrees that appeared, many were credited by Continental masonry with a Scottish title and/or origin (ie Ecossais), but with the possible odd exception, none were in any way connected with Scotland. While the bulk of degrees proved to be shallow and transient, others have survived to the present day, highly prized and sought after by many zealous adherents of freemasonry. A study of the rise of additional masonic degrees will show that if a degree contained anything of real value it survived; if not it vanished from the masonic scene.

Thus it transpired that all who wished to cultivate these additional degrees, were obliged by the edict of United Grand Lodge to work them as separate organisations, quite apart from the Craft; it is not surprising. therefore, that kindred and progressive degrees subsequently became grouped together and from this grouping arose the various masonic orders which in time evolved their own ruling bodies complete with their Laws and Constitutions. In an effort to obtain an accurate assessment of the total number of masonic degrees extant in England today, one would find that individual analysis would vary; but it is not unreasonable to estimate that commencing with the Entered Apprentice a zealous brother, possessing the requisite time, finance and ready acceptance, could conceivably advance through more than 110 degrees and this total could be supplemented by a further 15 or more, where separate secrets confined to the 'Chair' are communicated. Today the degree of Mark Master Mason is still adjudged by many to be the completion of the Fellowcraft degree, while the Holy Royal Arch is likewise considered to be the consummation of the Master Mason degree; and it is interesting to note that brethren holding high rank in the Craft enjoy equally high standing in other masonic Orders.

Masonry in its essence is a ceremonial method of approach to truth and it is beyond dispute that most degrees have a distinct lesson to impart, with an inner meaning to their ceremonies. Some are deemed to be more important than others, possessing special and peculiar value and embodying a highly developed form of symbolism, but an accumulation of degrees by no means implies an increase in real knowledge for investigation proves that what is regarded as pure masonry can be found in the degrees of Antient Craft Masonry and all other rites and degrees are no more than amplifications and elaborations, serving to throw a revealing light upon the content of the symbolic degrees, and therefore it is most important that we never lose sight of the allegiance due to our Mother Craft Lodge, whence we derived our masonic birth and infant nurture.

In compiling this book I have striven to maintain a high standard of accuracy, yet I appreciate that it is virtually impossible to produce a volume of this type without making some slight error or giving a certain interpretation, thereby provoking some form of criticism. My greatest hope is that all who enter the various masonic Orders may indeed find the light they seek, as there is virtually no end to the knowledge hidden within; but it is brotherhood absolute and inviolate which is the living inspiration of freemasonry.

Note

To enable the reader to progress smoothly through the information relative to each Order, the details have been conveniently sectionalised as follows:

HISTORY and ORIGIN: Here is compiled a brief résumé of the history of the particular Order.

STRUCTURE and QUALIFICATION: This section supplies a detailed list of officers applicable to subordinate bodies of the Order, describing the prerequisite qualifications for membership.

(*Optional offices are marked with an asterisk.)

REGALIA: All the various items of regalia worn in subordinate bodies are itemised under this heading and further enhanced by illustrations. Descriptions of Provincial regalia also refers to District and London ranks where applicable.

THE DEGREES: Each degree is reviewed separately in every possible case and a brief outline of the basic teachings of the grade are given.

It should be noted that the order in which the various degrees are printed in no way infers any order of progression or seniority.

The Holy Royal Arch

HISTORY and ORIGIN

The history of the Royal Arch is a complex one as the date at which it came into being as a separate degree cannot be ascertained with absolute accuracy. The first instance of the words 'Royal Arch' appearing in print, was the report of a public ceremonial procession in Ireland in 1743, when an arch described as 'Royal' was carried by two 'Excellents'. In the same year a book written by a Dr Dassigny referred to the misdeeds of a certain gentleman who claimed to be a Master of the Royal Arch from the city of York and who falsely proceeded to admit Irish brethren into this 'excellent part of masonry', but was eventually unmasked as an impostor through the offices of a brother who had recently attained the degree in London. The earliest reference to the Royal Arch in the minutes of a Lodge is again found in Ireland, in 1752, while the oldest record of an admission is that of 22 December 1757 when three brethren were 'raised to the degree of the Holy Royal Arch' in Fredericksburg, Virginia.

It is generally asserted that the Royal Arch was practised as an appendage to the Third Degree for many years, for it was regarded by the Antients as a fourth degree and they conferred it in their Lodges under the sanction of their own charter. The attitude of the Moderns, however, was very different for the degree, if worked, was certainly performed unofficially without the blessing of the Premier Grand Lodge and in time this led to the formation of separate Royal Arch Chapters. In July 1766 the Charter of Compact was signed and by that document the Grand and Royal Chapter of the Royal Arch of Jerusalem (the direct parent of the Supreme Grand Chapter of today) was constituted, but it was not until the Union that it was declared to be an official and universally accepted part of pure Antient Masonry. One of the important regulations promulgated by the new Grand Chapter required, that in acknowledging all Chapters in existence before 1813, each should attach itself to a regularly warranted Craft lodge and assume its number; thereby the present system came into being. Prior to the Union of 1813 it was necessary for all candidates, both Antient and Modern, to have previously served as Master of a lodge. As this condition seriously restricted the intake of members a ceremony of Installed Master was devised, whereby the candidate was created a virtual Past Master by 'passing the chair'. In 1823 the Supreme Grand Chapter altered the qualification to that of being a Master Mason with one year's standing and in 1893 the period was reduced to four weeks. With a history that goes back to the very early days of Masonry, the Royal Arch has been variously described as 'the most sacred part of Masonry' and 'the root, heart and marrow of Masonry'. Over this long period it has become the most talked of, and written about, degree in Freemasonry and for most is still regarded as the ultimate of the Craft system.

STRUCTURE and QUALIFICATION
Meetings of a Royal Arch chapter are called Convocations and the office structure is as follows:

First Principal (Z)
Second Principal (H)
Third Principal (J)
Scribe E (Secretary)
Scribe N
Treasurer
*Director of Ceremonies
*Almoner
*Charity Steward
Principal Sojourner

First Assistant Sojourner
Second Assistant Sojourner
*Assistant Director of Ceremonies
*Organist
*Assistant Scribe E
*Stewards
Janitor
*-*Permissive*

Freemasons wishing to be 'exalted' to this supreme degree must have been a Master Mason for a minimum of one month. There is also the additional qualification (apart from serving in certain senior offices in the chapter) that a candidate for the chair of Principal must also be an Installed Master in the Craft; this qualification is obligatory and cannot be waived by dispensation.

While it is possible that a chapter does not necessarily bear the same name as the lodge to which it is affiliated, it must, however, use the same number.

REGALIA

The regalia of this degree comprises an apron, sash and breast jewel. The apron is of white lamb skin having a triangular flap bordered with a two-inch ribbon of indented crimson and dark blue. In the centre of the flap is a triangle of white silk having a gilt border and three *taus* therein. Finally there are two tassels of gold suspended by white ribbons from beneath the flap.

The sash is worn over the left shoulder and features a double indented crimson and dark blue design, having a silk fringe and similar triangular emblem (to that on the flap) at the point.

The breast jewel of gilt or gold depicts a double triangle within a circle, having in the centre an emblem of the All-seeing Eye, this being suspended by a white ribbon. Officers of a chapter wear a collar of crimson ribbon four inches wide, with the appropriate jewel set in a triangle suspended therefrom.

Present and Past Principals: Similar regalia is worn, with the exception that the background colour to the triangular motifs on the apron flap and point of the sash is changed to crimson, as are the tassel and breast jewel ribbons. The fringe to the sash is now changed from crimson and dark blue to gold.

Provincial Officers: Once again similar regalia is worn with the distinguishing colour now being that of dark blue, with the addition of the badge of office being appended to the centre of the apron below the flap. A provincial collar of dark blue, crimson and light blue, two inches in width, with the appropriate jewel suspended therefrom is also worn, while the breast jewel features a narrow tricoloured ribbon of similar colours.

Grand Officers: Here we have the introduction of a four-inch double indented crimson and royal blue border to the apron, with the emblem of office displayed in the centre within two branches of gilt embroidered laurel. The distinguishing colour to the backing and ribbon is again dark blue, while the sash and breast jewel are identical to those of a Provincial Officer.

THE DEGREE

Described as the perfection and completion of all Freemasonry, this degree deals with a lengthy period following the close of King Solomon's glorious reign. The temple of Jerusalem had been destroyed, the kingdom of Judea divided and the tribes taken into captivity. Babylon eventually fell to Cyrus the Great, to become part of the mighty Persian empire and this remarkably humane ruler liberated the Jewish captives and invited them to return to Jerusalem to commence the rebuilding of the Temple. This legend sets out to restore the genuine secrets of a Master Mason and this is accomplished by workmen who make a momentous discovery during their labours and from this a most interesting and illuminating explanation of the nature of God is conveyed.

Mark Masonry

HISTORY and ORIGIN

While there is evidence that a form of Mark degree was extant in Scotland as early as 1599, according to earliest known English records, Mark masonry was introduced in a speculative body at Portsmouth on 1 September 1769 at Royal Arch Chapter No 257, when Thomas Dunckerley made certain brethren Mark Masons and Mark Masters, each choosing his mark.

This degree was subsequently worked in many lodges and even under the authority of the old Grand Lodge at York, but the effect of the Union in 1813 between the Antients and Moderns was the specific recognition of the three Craft degrees only, including the Holy Royal Arch and thus completely excluding the Mark degree. Nevertheless many lodges continued to work the degree and while the original circumstances would appear to have been detrimental to Mark masonry, they were eventually to cause several leading Mark masons to found their own Grand Mark Lodge in June 1856, with Lord Leigh as the first Grand Master.

Happily by 1860 a Concordat establishing a common ceremonial was entered into by the English Grand Mark Lodge and the Grand Chapter of Scotland and slowly this degree grew in popularity to make it together with the Royal Arch one of the most successfully supported degrees in freemasonry. Today there are over 1,550 Mark lodges under the English Constitution and it is interesting to note that a vast number of brethren who have attained eminence in the Craft have been no less eminent in the Mark.

STRUCTURE and QUALIFICATION

The officers of a Mark lodge are:

Worshipful Master
Senior Warden
Junior Warden
Master Overseer
Senior Overseer
Junior Overseer
*Chaplain
Treasurer
Registrar of Marks
Secretary
*Director of Ceremonies
Senior Deacon
Junior Deacon
*Assistant Director of Ceremonies
*Almoner
*Organist
*Assistant Secretary
Inner Guard
*Stewards
Tyler

Every candidate to be advanced to the degree of Mark Master Mason must be a Master Mason of a regular and recognised Craft lodge, while candidates for the office of Worshipful Master must nominally have first served as Worshipful Master of a Craft lodge, although a dispensation is commonly obtainable which obviates this prior condition.

REGALIA

Members of the degree are required to wear aprons of white kid having a triangular flap, all bordered with two-inch ribbon of light blue with crimson edges; the apron has three rosettes of similar colouring.

Masters and Past Masters have the rosettes replaced by silver levels, similar to those worn in the Craft.

The jewel of the degree is a keystone of ivory or other approved material having a silver lewis: this is suspended from a silver bar by one-inch ribbon in the colours of the Order. Each face of the keystone bears certain characters or letters which have particular significance to the wearer.

Officers of a lodge wear collars four inches broad in crimson and sky blue, from which is suspended the emblem of their office superimposed on a silver keystone, approximately three inches in length.

Provincial Grand Officers wear aprons decorated with four-inch ribbon having a royal blue centre and crimson edges. The emblem of office is contained within a garter which bears the name of the province or district: this is situated on the centre of the apron below the flap. The breast jewel is the familiar keystone but with gilt fittings and the darker blue ribbon. A four-inch matching collar is also worn and from this hangs the jewel of office which if acting rank will consist of the emblem of office surmounting a circle and if past rank will be an oval garter bearing the name of province or district with the emblem of office in the centre.

Grand Officers regalia is identical in colouring to that of a provincial Grand Officer but the emblem of office on the apron is surrounded by a wreath of rose leaves and hyssop with three levels all in gold. The matching collar is four inches wide and is decorated with rose leaves and hyssop.

THE DEGREE

The ceremony of admission is called 'advancement' and chronologically the degree follows that of Fellow Craft (as it does in Scotland). It is one of the oldest and most interesting grades of freemasonry and today incorporates two degrees, for the candidate is first acknowledged as a Mark Man and subsequently advanced as a Mark Master Mason in the same ceremony. It appears that the degree grew out of an ancient ceremony in which each craftsman selected for himself a private mark with which he might designate his particular work and this mark was duly registered with the constituted authority. The legend of the degree is singularly instructive and well founded on statements of Holy Writ, relating to a period in the building of the Temple prior to the death of Hiram Abiff; it teaches the lesson that education is the reward of labour and contains a dramatic message, that fraud can never succeed. As stated, the symbol of the degree is a keystone on which is engraved certain mystic letters, the meaning of which is revealed during the ceremony.

Mark Master Mason breast jewel.

HISTORY and ORIGIN

While the statutes of a self-styled Grand Lodge of Royal Ark Mariners produced in 1871 mention that '. . . in the year 1772 a Grand Lodge was reconstituted', this evidence is not generally accepted as reliable.

The first authentic record of the degree appears in the minutes of a meeting held in Bath in 1790, while numerous records exist throughout the country of 'elevations' since that date. This degree however was to experience great difficulties and it was many years before a serious revival of Ark Masonry took place, but in 1816 a Brother John F. Dorrington awakened a renewed interest in the degree when he became Grand Commander. It was this revival that eventually stimulated the Grand Lodge of Mark Master Masons to take decisive action by placing the degree under its protection.

A Grand Master's Royal Ark Council was formed to regulate the degree and the first original working under the new constitutions was effected in Mother Lodge of Royal Ark Mariners No 1 in 1872. Since then the fraternity has grown apace and lodges of this degree have spread throughout the world; today there are over 830 lodges working under the English Constitution.

STRUCTURE and QUALIFICATION

Bodies are called Lodges, each of which assumes the number of the Mark Lodge to which it is attached. Officers of a lodge are comprised as follows:

> Worshipful Commander (N)
> Senior Warden (J)

Junior Warden (S)
*Chaplain
Treasurer
Scribe
*Director of Ceremonies
Senior Deacon
Junior Deacon
*Assistant Director of Ceremonies
*Organist
Guardian
*Stewards
Warder

The qualification for 'elevation to membership' is, not surprisingly, that of being a Mark Master Mason, while in all cases a dispensation is required where a candidate for the chair of Worshipful Commander has not previously held the office of Worshipful Master of a lodge of Mark Master Masons.

The Royal Ark Mariner Degree does not have a Provincial or District structure of officers, but is governed by the respective administration controlling the Mark Lodges within the given area.

The breast jewel worn by members of Royal Ark Mariner lodges. The ribbon depicts the colours of the rainbow.

REGALIA

The regalia comprises an apron of white kid having a segmental flap, all bordered with rainbow ribbon one inch and a quarter in width and having three rosettes of similar ribbon. The apron of a Commander is identical, save that the rosettes are replaced by triangles of silver.

The jewel is a segmental plate of silver representing a rainbow from which is suspended a dove bearing an olive branch in its beak; this is suspended from a rainbow ribbon and silver bar. The name and number of the Lodge may be inscribed on an oval plate fastened to the ribbon. Past Commanders may also wear a jewel featuring the initial N within a triangle pendant from a similar ribbon.

Lodges provide collars for the use of officers and these are of rainbow ribbon four inches broad with silver button and cord, to which the respective emblem of office is attached.

Holders of Provincial Grand Rank wear a one-and-a-quarter-inch collarette in the colours of the order from which is suspended a silver triangle bearing a representation of the Ark. **Holders of Grand Rank** wear a similar collarette except that it has a golden button and vertical braid at the apex; the jewel is also gilt as are the apron triangles and breast jewel if worn.

THE DEGREE

Elevation into this degree commemorates the providence and mercy of God and relates to the legend of the Deluge: the subject matter being taken direct from the VSL, is naturally both beautiful and instructive. When he enters the Temple, the attention of the candidate is directed to three pillars and at a certain stage the Ark is momentarily symbolised in terms similar to the ark of salvation. He is finally instructed to advance in the spirit of the cardinal virtues. An interesting facet of this degree is the positioning of the Wardens as in an old Craft lodge.

Order of the Secret Monitor

HISTORY and ORIGIN
While the first references to the Order of David and Jonathan are known to be of Dutch origin, the Secret Monitor arose in America as a side degree conferred by any mason who had received it himself. It was brought to England by Dr I. Zacharie when he returned from America (following the Civil War) around 1875. Under his leadership a Grand Council was formed in 1887 and the ritual was extended when a further two degrees were added, one of which pertained to the chair of Supreme Ruler.

The degrees gained in popularity, but this success was to bring about a series of unfortunate events, for in the meantime the Grand Council of Allied Masonic Degrees had been empowered by an American body (of similar name) to confer their version of the degree. This resulted in the Allied body denouncing the Grand Council of the Order of the Secret Monitor and attempting to assume sole jurisdiction over the degree, but in spite of this Dr Zacharie's group prospered. Regretfully a period of over 37 years elapsed, during which both orders were conferring a Secret Monitor degree, but the matter was finally resolved in 1931 when C. W. Napier-Clavering was in the favourable position of being Grand Supreme Ruler and also Grand Master of Allied Masonry. He then implemented an agreement transferring all rights to the Grand Council of the Order of the Secret Monitor and the degree was removed from the list of degrees of the Allied body.

The Order comprises of the following degrees:

1. Secret Monitor
2. Prince
3. Supreme Ruler

STRUCTURE and QUALIFICATION

In this Order we find that assemblies are termed Conclaves, each with a Supreme Ruler at its head. The Visiting Deacons are officers with a special function peculiar to this degree. It is laid down that they should afford assistance and support to a brother in time of sorrow and distress and they should also search out and warn him if he be exposed to danger, secret or apparent.

The structure of officers is as follows:

Supreme Ruler	*Assistant Director of
Counsellor	Ceremonies
Guide	*Organist
*Chaplain	*Assistant Secretary
Treasurer	*Scroll Bearer
Secretary	Guarder
Director of Ceremonies	*Stewards
Visiting Deacons (usually four)	Sentinel

In the Second degree the regular officers are:

David (SR)
Jonathan (IPSR)
Abishai
Adino
Eleazar
Shammah
*Lecturer

There is only the single qualification of Master Mason for prospective candidates for this Order.

REGALIA

Regalia of the First degree comprises a jewel in gilt, being two equilateral triangles interlaced with three arrows and charged with the letters D and J. It is suspended from a ribbon in the colours of the Order, ie purple—orange—purple.

Officers wear a crimson sash four inches wide and having a gold fringe below the frog, which also features two interlaced triangles in metal gilt.

In the Princes (Second) degree an identical jewel is worn, but it is suspended from a ribbon of equal stripes, orange—purple—orange. The sash of office is four inches wide with a purple selvage, having two outer orange stripes and two inner purple stripes with a central crimson stripe one-eighth of an inch wide. The frog also bears the interlaced triangle motif with a gold fringe.

Second Degree members breast jewel for the Order of Secret Monitor.

A Supreme Ruler wears the jewel of the Order suspended from a collarette in the colours of the Second degree, together with the appropriate sash bearing the initials SR in silver and a purple robe with orange or gold facings.

Provincial Grand Officers wear a sash of empire blue bearing a gold embroidered motif of the Order on the breast, together with initials designating the office of the holder and finished with a gold fringe. A collarette two inches wide is worn, also of Empire blue from which is suspended a gilt jewel bearing the name of the Province and the title of office.

Grand Officers wear a four-inch sash of crimson, bordered with gold cord and bearing a gilt embroidered celestial crown above the initials designating the office and beneath the interlaced triangle motif of the Order, together with a gold fringe. The appropriate jewel is a gilt oval bearing the title of office and is suspended from a one-inch collarette of Indian yellow and crimson.

THE DEGREES

Secret Monitor—First degree: The legend narrated during the Induction ceremony is the story of the remarkable friendship which existed between David and Jonathan. During the ceremony the candidate is instructed in a certain course of action to be adopted when a brother is about to do anything which might prove injurious to himself and it teaches a beautiful lesson in friendship and fidelity.

Prince—Second degree: The admission ceremony to an assembly of Princes is also derived from the Book of Samuel and narrates how Saul sought the life of David. It further relates an interesting legend of the methods contrived to thwart the efforts of the jealous King.

Supreme Ruler—Third degree: This last named degree is unusual in that the ceremony of Installation constitutes the third degree of the Order pertaining to the Kingship of David and is fundamentally concerned with the headship of a Conclave. Embodied in the ritual of this degree, however, is the ceremony of commissioning, which gives rank and status within the Order as a whole, a certificate being issued to that effect.

Royal and Select Masters

HISTORY and ORIGIN

The Grand Council of Royal and Select Masters of England and Wales etc, was formally constituted on 29 July 1873 by four Councils chartered just two years earlier by the Grand Council of New York. They organised themselves into a sovereign body under the patronage of the Rev Canon G. R. Portal, Past Grand Master of the Grand Lodge of Mark Master Masons, who was installed as the Grand Master of the Order.

This Grand Council had its vicissitudes but continues to prosper and today has many Councils overseas which are controlled by District Grand Councils. The degrees in this group are frequently referred to as 'Cryptic Degrees' but this description is not strictly correct, as only two actually refer to a crypt. It is somewhat surprising to note that to many, these ceremonies constitute nothing more than interesting side degrees or a random collection of unrelated incidents in the story of KST, but to the serious and understanding masonic student, they prove to be the essential link between the degrees of Master Mason and Royal Arch Mason.

Administered from Mark Masons' Hall, Grand Council governs over 160 Councils and exercises authority over the following degrees:

1. Select Master
2. Royal Master
3. Most Excellent Master
4. Super-Excellent Master

STRUCTURE and QUALIFICATION

Bodies are called Councils and have a compliment of officers comprising of:

Thrice Illustrious Master
Deputy Master
Principal Conductor of the Work
Treasurer
Recorder
*Director of Ceremonies
Captain of the Guard
Conductor of the Council
*Assistant Director of Ceremonies
*Organist
Steward
*Manciples
Sentinel

The statutory qualifications for membership are those of Mark Master Mason and Royal Arch Mason.

REGALIA

The regalia of this order is unique and consists of a triangular

Royal and Select members breast jewel.

apron of white kid with crimson ribbed silk, two inches wide and trimmed with gold braid around the edges. There is a semi-circular flap with similar trimmings. Masters and Past Masters have similar aprons with the appropriate badge embroidered in the centre. The jewel is a skeleton equilateral triangle of white enamel, with point downwards and surmounted by an imperial crown in gold suspended from a crimson ribbon. Officers of private Councils wear a collar of crimson silk four inches wide from which is suspended a gilt trowel interlaced with the emblem of office.

Provincial and District Grand Officers wear aprons with an embroidered badge of office in the centre within a garter bearing the name of the province or district. A four-inch wide matching collar is also worn from which is suspended the jewel of office. Grand Officers wear similar aprons and collars trimmed with gold lace, while Divisional and District Inspectors also wear a Chain of Office.

THE DEGREES
On all occasions the business of private councils is transacted in the degree of Select Master. Lodges of Most Excellent Masters, Councils of Royal Masters and Councils of Super-Excellent Masters are opened only to admit candidates.

Select Master: This degree is supposedly held in the secret vault which has been constructed beneath the Temple, consisting of several arches, into one of which the secrets were deposited and later discovered. It relates how a well-known mason employed by KS accidentally intrudes into the crypt where the three GMs were wont to meet and confer, and illustrates the consequence of this intrusion. The symbolic colours are red and black. (A similar legend may be found in the Allied group and is also in one of the degrees under the A & A Rite.)

Royal Master: This degree is set in time just prior to the completion and dedication of the first Temple; it highlights the completed vessels pertaining to the House of the Lord and refers to a certain fellow craft making diligent enquiry of HA as to when he might receive the secrets of a MM. The subsequent disquisition by our Grand Master on the subject of death is one of the most enthralling pieces of ritual in freemasonry. It also shows how the secrets came to be deposited in the crypt where they were subsequently found. The symbolic colours are black and red.

Most Excellent Master: This degree deals with the completion and dedication of the first Temple; it celebrates the completion of the whole edifice and mentions the installation of the Ark of the Covenant in the Holy Place. It constitutes a fitting ceremonial and dramatic preface to the Cryptic Degrees. The symbolic colour of the degree is purple.

Super-Excellent Master: The legend around which this degree is built brings the story of the first Temple down to the time of its imminent destruction and refers to the siege of Jerusalem by the troops of the enraged Nebuchadnezzar, following the rebellion of the tributary Jewish king, Zedekiah. The symbolic colour of the degree is crimson.

Order of the
Allied Masonic Degrees

HISTORY and ORIGIN

The Grand Council of the Allied Masonic Degrees was formed in 1879 to bring under its direction all lodges of various orders who recognised no central authority and were not regulated by the other major governing bodies. Initially the degrees of Grand High Priest, St Lawrence the Martyr, the Red Cross of Babylon and Knights of Constantinople placed themselves under the control of this body and by 1897 the degrees of Grand Tilers of Solomon, one degree of the Secret Monitor and the Order of Holy Wisdom (Knight Templar Priest grades) had also been included. Eventually, however, in 1923 a Grand College of Holy Royal Arch Knight Templar Priests for England was erected at Newcastle and the Grand Council accordingly disclaimed control of this large group of degrees. Following this in 1931 the Grand Council of Allied Masonic Degrees agreed to cease working their single degree of the Secret Monitor and so today private Councils of the Order are empowered to work the degrees of:

> St Lawrence the Martyr
> Knight of Constantinople
> Grand Tilers of Solomon
> Red Cross of Babylon
> Grand High Priest

In 1972 the title of this body was changed to the Grand Council of the Order of the Allied Masonic Degrees and today there are in excess of 150 Councils ranged under its banner.

St Lawrence the Martyr	Knight of Constantinople	Grand Tilers of Solomon	Red Cross of Babylon Royal Arch Chapter	Persian Court	Grand High Priest
Wor Master	Illustrious Potentate	Wor Master	Revd Prelate	Th III Sovereign	M E President
S Warden	Chief of Builders	S Warden	2nd Principal	Master of Household	Vice President
J Warden	Chief of Artizans	J Warden	—	Master of Cavalry	—
*Chaplain	—	—	Chaplain	—	Chaplain
Treasurer	—	—	—	—	—
Secretary					
Dir Ceremonies	Dir Ceremonies	Dir Ceremonies	Dir Ceremonies	Dir Ceremonies	Master Ceremonies
S Deacon	S Conductor	Conductor	Jewish Guide	Master of Infantry	Conductor
J Deacon	J Conductor	Capt of Host	—	—	Herald
*ADC	ADC	ADC	ADC	ADC	ADC
*Almoner	—	—	—	—	—
*Organist	—	—	—	—	—
Inner Guard	Guarder	—	Capt Temple Guard	Capt Persian Guard	Steward
*Steward 1	—	—	1st Jewish Guard	1st Persian Guard	—
*Steward 2	—	—	2nd Jewish Guard	2nd Persian Guard	—
Tyler	Sentinel	Tyler	Sentinel	Sentinel	Sentinel

STRUCTURE and QUALIFICATION

In a Council of the Allied Masonic Degrees we find that the office structure varies from degree to degree as shown in the accompanying chart on p. 29.

The degree of St Lawrence the Martyr is that in which all administrative work is carried out, candidates are admitted to the Order and the Installation of the Worshipful Master takes place. Prospective candidates for admission must be of the rank of Master Mason, Mark Master Mason and Royal Arch Mason.

Special note: The degree of Red Cross of Babylon is worked in two parts, the first being in a Royal Arch Council and the second in a Persian Court. Allied Councils are grouped into Divisions which are administered by a Divisional Grand Prefect.

REGALIA

The regalia of the Order comprises breast jewels, the details of which are listed below; they are worn as miniatures suspended from a bar by ribbons of appropriate colours.

The jewels of the Order of Allied Masonic Degrees. Left to right, St Lawrence the Martyr, Red Cross of Babylon, Knight of Constantinople, Grand Tilers of Solomon and Grand High Priest.

At the meeting of Grand Council in October 1981, amendments to the constitutions were promulgated allowing brethren who have acquired all the degrees to wear a composite jewel in place of the standard miniatures. Being gold in colour, it is pentagonal in shape and incorporates symbols of the five degrees and is suspended from a plain thistle green ribbon worn on the left breast.

St Lawrence the Martyr: A gridiron in silver, suspended by a ribbon orange in the centre, bordered on each side with royal blue. A Past Master's Gridiron is enclosed in a circle.

Knight of Constantinople: A Maltese cross surmounted by a crescent both in gold, suspended by a green ribbon on which are three poignards in gold pointing downward. (Plymouth Councils have a jewel of special design.)

Grand Tilers of Solomon: A triangle in black enamel edged with gold, inscribed on the obverse with the number 27 in Hebrew characters and on the reverse with the Ineffable Name in the Cabalistic Order, suspended by a ribbon, fiery red in the centre, bordered on each side with pale grey and surmounted by three crowns in gilt. On the ribbon is a hand grasping a poignard pointing downward, in gilt.

Red Cross of Babylon: A gold seven-pointed star with gold crossed swords on a green enamel circle in the centre, suspended by a green ribbon.

Grand High Priest: A mitre on a triangle, both in gold suspended by a red ribbon.

Officers of Councils wear a collar in the colours of the degree of St Lawrence the Martyr, being of orange silk four inches wide with a one-inch border of royal blue on each side. From this collar is suspended the silver emblem of office (as in the Craft) superimposed on a gridiron within a circle, bearing the name of the Council.

Past Masters: The pentagonal jewel is worn suspended from a plain thistle green collarette, one inch wide.

Divisional, London & Overseas Rank: The pentagonal jewel is worn suspended from a two-inch wide thistle green collarette.

Grand Officers: Holders of this rank wear a thistle green collar four inches wide which is edged with gold lace and bears an attractive embroidered design of oak leaves and acorns, while a representation of the seal of the Order is suspended from the point of the collar. The Grand Master, his deputy and Divisional Grand Prefects wear chains. The Undress collar is plain thistle green.

Plymouth Councils: The special regalia of Plymouth Councils comprises of a composite apron of thistle green complete with triangular flap and bordered with ribbon woven in the ribbon colours of the degrees of St Lawrence the Martyr, Grand Tilers of Solomon and Secret Monitor (old AMD colours, see below). The flap bears a silver gridiron (St Lawrence the Martyr), while in the centre of the apron is a St Andrew's Cross (Red Cross of Babylon) superimposed on a Passion Cross (Knights of Constantinople) both embroidered in red silk and charged with a jewish mitre in gold (Grand High Priest). A Past Master of the Order has the addition of two silver plates featuring a square upon a gridiron surrounded by a circle, which are fixed in the normal position of the two lower taus on a Craft Past Master's apron. The breast jewel pertains to the degree of Knight of Constantinople and consists of a six-pointed star of silver which bears a golden heart pierced by two daggers and inscribed with the word Excelsior. It is suspended by a Burgundy red ribbon which bears a Passion cross of silver in the centre with the top bar in the shape of a crescent.

THE DEGREES

St Lawrence the Martyr: The actual date when this ritual was introduced is not known, but it is believed to have been worked in England two centuries ago. It is generally accepted to be the remnants of an old operative ceremony originating from Lancashire and designed to distinguish the true craftsman from the speculative mason. While having little masonic connection, the interesting legend relates to the martyrdom of St Lawrence who was afterwards canonised for his fidelity and Christian attributes. Understandably the lesson taught is fortitude.

Knight of Constantinople: This degree is an authentic 'side degree', where it was customary for one brother to confer it on another and while it is known to have been working in America in 1831, its actual origin is unknown. The ritual attempts to connect the legendary Constantine with the masonic fraternity and teaches a fine lesson in universal equality and humility; it also incorporates a suggestion of operative influence in an extensive lecture which also imbues the lesson of justice.

Grand Tilers of Solomon: Under an early title of Select Masters of Twenty Seven, this degree is known to date back in America to 1893. It is very similar in character to the degree of Select Master and relates the story of the accidental intrusion of a craftsman into the secret vault of KS, where his fate is determined by the three GMs. This degree was conferred on the Earl of Euston, the Grand Master of Allied Masonic Degrees, in 1893 with powers to propagate it in England and accordingly it was incorporated under the Grand Council of the Allied Masonic Degrees.

Red Cross of Babylon: This degree is of considerable antiquity, being closely associated with the Holy Royal Arch and the rebuilding of the second Temple of Jerusalem with the candidate bearing the name of Zerubbabel. The legend beginning in the days of Cyrus, King of Persia, continues through to the time of Darius and incorporates an outstanding feature of passing a bridge over a river which has particular significance. The degree culminates with an intricate debate taken from the First Book of Esdras which established the profound maxim 'great is truth'. In Scotland this degree is found as the Babylonish Pass while in America it is annexed to the Templar grades. In both Ireland and America it also constitutes the Order of Knight Masons.

Grand High Priest: This is an amalgamation of two degrees originating from Germany and France in the middle of the 18th century and was worked extensively in America around

1802, being in many cases a perquisite or honorary degree conferred on those who have presided as, or are elected to the chair of, First Principal of a Holy Royal Arch Chapter. In England there was ample evidence of this Holy Order when the Grand Council was formed in 1879 and was one of the first Orders to place itself under its aegis.

The degree is founded on the Blessing of Abraham and the consecration of Aaron, and the candidate is admitted by the President (who represents the King of Salem) and set apart with due ceremonial to the Holy office of Grand High Priest in a most beautiful and uplifting enactment. It is usual that this degree is only performed in any Council once in every year although this is not a rigid ruling.

Knights of Constantinople—Plymouth Working: In 1865 a Council of Knights of Constantinople was formed at Devonport, Plymouth and from the St Aubyn Council (now No 33 TI on the Allied Masonic Degrees roll) several other Councils were warranted: at Truro (1866), Chatham (1866), Hong Kong (1866), Gibraltar (1868), Bristol (1878) and Plymouth (1874 and 1907). In 1910, the three remaining Councils situated in Plymouth Nos 33, 34 and 35, conceded to the Grand Council of the Allied Masonic Degrees, but in so doing obtained for themselves the exclusive privilege of continuing to wear their own distinctive apron and also the right to confer the degree as practised by Plymouth Councils since 1865. The degree embodies the principle of humility and equality and possesses some interesting elements not found elsewhere.

Special demonstrations of the Plymouth Working for which only Christian brethren are eligible, have been given from time to time, held before the meetings of the Grand Council in London at the invitation of the Grand Master.

The Ancient and Accepted Rite for England and Wales

HISTORY and ORIGIN

While some of the degrees within this Rite may have had an earlier origin, the Rite as such appears to have germinated around the early 1760s when a list of 25 degrees were drawn up, several of which were probably in name only. While there were various rival bodies controlling Rites of so-called Scottish degrees, it was the Grand Lodge of France in conjunction with the Council of Knights of the East who deputed Stephen Morin to promulgate Masonry in the West Indies, and from his labours Scottish Rite Masonry in America took its footing. By about 1765 a Rite of Perfection of 25 degrees was being practised both in Continental Europe and the Americas, and

Collar and jewel worn by members of the eighteenth Rose Croix degree.

towards the end of the century the Rite was increased to 33 degrees. In 1801 a Supreme Council was formed in Charleston, South Carolina and in 1819 a patent was granted to the Duke of Sussex to form a Supreme Council in England, but he failed to act upon it, probably due to his keen desire to see the United Grand Lodge consolidate its 'purist' policy, which of course excluded all chivalric degrees, because from around 1775 the Rose Croix degree had been worked as a final or 'ne plus ultra' degree of most English Knight Templar encampments. It was not until 1845 that the Supreme Council for England and Wales was formed and eventually assumed control of all independent Rose Croix degrees. The degrees of the Rite are:

1–3. Not worked by the Supreme Council
4. Secret Master
5. Perfect Master
6. Intimate Secretary
7. Provost & Judge
8. Intendant of the Buildings
9. Elect of Nine
10. Elect of Fifteen
11. Sublime Elect
12. Grand Master Architect
13. Royal Arch (of Enoch)
14. Scotch Knight of Perfection
15. Knight of the Sword or of the East
16. Prince of Jerusalem
17. Knight of the East & West
18. Knight of the Pelican and Eagle and Sovereign Prince Rose Croix of H.R.D.M.
19. Grand Pontiff
20. Venerable Grand Master
21. Patriarch Noachite
22. Prince of Libanus
23. Chief of the Tabernacle
24. Prince of the Tabernacle
25. Knight of the Brazen Serpent
26. Prince of Mercy
27. Commander of the Temple
28. Knight of the Sun
29. Knight of St Andrew
30. Grand Elected Knight K.H., Knight of the Black and White Eagle
31. Grand Inspector Inquisitor Commander
32. Sublime Prince of the Royal Secret
33. Sovereign Grand Inspector General

It is normal for one or two of the intermediate degrees (4°–17°) to be demonstrated in full every year; understandably such meetings are very well supported. Today there are in excess of 860 Chapters owing allegiance to this sovereign body, and while the majority are situated in England and Wales the Supreme Council has warranted chapters of this Order in over 20 different countries.

STRUCTURE and QUALIFICATION

All general business of the Order is transacted in assemblies described as Rose Croix Chapters. There is an interesting office structure as follows:

> Most Wise Sovereign
> Prelate
> First General
> Second General
> Treasurer
> Recorder
> Director of Ceremonies
> Marshal
> Raphael
> Almoner
> Herald
> Captain of the Guard
> *Organist
> *Assistant Recorder
> *Assistant Director of Ceremonies
> *Stewards
> Outer Guard

Membership is usually by invitation and may only be considered from Master Masons of at least one year's standing who profess the Christian faith. A Chapter takes the candidate as far as the 18° of the Rite.

REGALIA

18° Sovereign Prince Rose Croix: Members wear a collar, four inches wide, of rose pink edged with gold braid. The collar is richly embroidered with a crown of thorns and a serpent holding its tail in its mouth while at the apex there is a pelican feeding its young. The collar is reversible being black on the underside and adorned with three red crosses. The jewel suspended from the collar is a pair of compasses in gilt surmounted

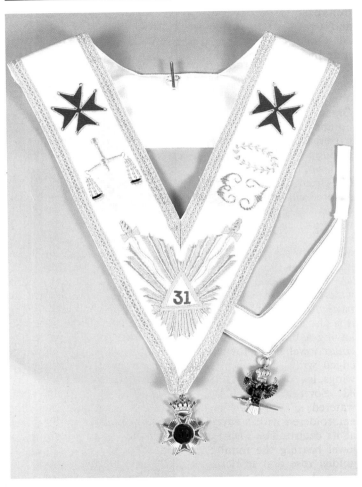

An English thirty-first collar of white watered silk and gold wire embroidery with star jewel attached and neck collarette and eagle jewel behind.

by a rose and celestial crown, depicting the pelican on one side and a silver eagle on the reverse.

30° Grand Elected Knight Kadosh: Consists of a black sash four inches wide, worn over the left shoulder, fringed with silver and embroidered with the emblems of the degree, ie an eagle displayed holding an anchor, the banners of England and Wales with that of the Supreme Council and a Teutonic Cross of red. The jewel is a cross Pateé in red enamel with the number 30 upon blue enamel in the centre and is worn on the left breast. From a collarette of black watered silk with silver edging is hung a black double-spreading eagle surmounted by a crown, holding a sword in its claws.

31° Grand Inspector Inquisitor Commander: A collar of white watered silk four inches wide embroidered with the emblems of the degree which include the 'scales of justice', and trimmed with gold lace. From this is suspended the cross, which is similar to the 30° cross, but bearing the number 31. A collarette of white is worn, from which is suspended an eagle of black, having wing-tips and tail of gilt.

32° Sublime Prince of the Royal Secret: A collar of black watered silk four and a half inches wide embroidered with the particular emblems of the degree and edged with silver lace; it is also reversible being of red watered silk on the underside having a black cross embroidered at the point in gold. The collar jewel bears the number 32 while a red silk collarette edged with gold supports a double eagle of black with the wings, legs, claws and outer tips of feathers in gilt.

33° Sovereign Grand Inspector General: A sash of white watered silk, five inches wide, edged with gold lace and embroidered with a rayed delta having the number 33 in red at its centre. The sash is worn over the left shoulder with a jewel bearing the number 33 appended at its base below a golden rose and scarlet bow. The eagle of silver and gilt is suspended from a black oxidised chain and a cap of black velvet is also worn, decorated with a triangular gilt badge bearing the number 33.

District: An Inspector General of a District, when a member of the 33°, has regalia similar to normal members of that grade save that the eagle is suspended from a silver chain and the triangular cap badge in gilt is mounted on a gilt circle.

Supreme Council: Members of the Supreme Council have the distinction of wearing their eagle from a golden chain and having a triple cross of red enamel suspended from the blade of the sword between the eagle claws. An eagle charged with a red enamelled triple cross is worn on the front of the cap.

Most Wise Sovereign: The Most Wise Sovereign of a Chapter, in addition to the regalia indicating the degree of the holder, wears a red enamelled Greek cross surmounted by a celestial crown from a rose coloured neck ribbon.

THE DEGREES

As the first three degrees of this Rite correspond with symbolic or Craft masonry, they are no longer worked as part of the Rite. The 4th to 17th degrees inclusive are conferred by name only while the 18th degree is worked in full.

18° Sovereign Prince Rose Croix: The ceremonies of this degree, while divided into four distinct sections, are of a most imposing and impressive character. The symbolic teaching is not only pleasing but also consistent with the Christian faith. In a series of highly mystical experiences, it expresses the figurative passage of man through the darkest vale, accompanied and sustained by the three theological virtues. The final reception of the candidate into the abode of light is accomplished with the recovery of the lost word. Progress beyond the 18th degree cannot be attained without the candidate being first installed as Most Wise Sovereign of a Chapter and completing at least three years as an 18th degree member. He may then be recommended for promotion to the 30th degree.

30° Grand Elected Knight Kadosh: Again the 19th to 29th degrees inclusive are conferred by name only. The attention of the candidate is particularly drawn to a philosophical interpretation of the masonic system and he is pledged to figuratively punish crime and protect innocence. The 30° Kadosh (signifying Holy or Consecrated) is strongly Templar in tone, vested with a mystical ladder symbolic of virtue and science.

Further advancement to the 31st and 32nd degrees is conferred on specially selected candidates in strictly limited numbers.

31° Grand Inspector Inquisitor Commander: This degree is conferred in a Supreme Tribunal wherein the candidate is able to estimate the real value of eternal masonic justice and equity. He is charged to oversee the observation of masonic laws and in the course of his induction is introduced to representatives of great law givers of the past.

32° Sublime Prince of the Royal Secret: This degree is one that counsels charity and tolerance towards all mankind. This is exemplified by a symbolic pilgrimage in search of truth, when the candidate is conducted around the Camp of Chivalry where the respective points mark one of the renowned philosophies or religions of the World. Here, within the Consistory, is hidden a mystery of great import and in its true interpretation the Royal Secret is to be found.

33° Sovereign Grand Inspector General: The supreme degree of the Rite incorporates a most impressive ceremony in which the candidate is required to endure a test demanding great courage, this being followed by a lengthy obligation and fitting climax, when he is married to the Order with a golden ring of special significance. The peculiar duties of members entail that they encourage charity and fraternal love throughout the Order and preserve with due reverence the dogmas, statutes and doctrines of the Rite.

Red Cross of Constantine

The full title of this Order is The Masonic and Military Order of the Red Cross of Constantine and the Orders of the Holy Sepulchre and of St John the Evangelist.

HISTORY and ORIGIN

The origin of this Order is surrounded by considerable mystery, for while mention is made of the 'Red Cross' degree as early as 1813, it would be negligent to assume that the Red Cross of Constantine was the degree in question, for there were a multiplicity of organisations around 1800 which had assumed the title of 'Red Cross of . . .', all with rituals propounding widely differing legends.

It is worthy of note, however, that Robert Carlile, who was fairly accurate in his revelations, published an 'Exposure' in 1825 which featured a degree called the Red Cross of Rome and Constantine, and the working, while being a very shortened version, is strikingly similar to that in use today. It is therefore not unreasonable to assume that the Red Cross of Constantine was being actively promoted in the early nineteenth century and even possibly the late 1700s; but it is now an accepted fact that the establishment of the Order as we know it, was the work of Robert Wentworth Little who supposedly reconstituted the Grand Council with the assistance of W. H. White (Grand Secretary of United Grand Lodge) and W. J. Hughan (the famous masonic historian) in 1865. While progress was initially slow, the Order nevertheless attracted a host of devoted adherents; not only did it take root in England, but it spread elsewhere with great rapidity and within eight years over 100 conclaves had been chartered, and by 1880 six new Sovereign Grand Conclaves or Councils had been formed by conclaves originally owing allegiance to England. Today there are over 300 conclaves on the roll of the Grand Imperial Conclave and happily this delightful Order continues to flourish.

The degrees controlled by this sovereign body are:

1. Knight of the Red Cross of Constantine
2. (a) Knight of the Holy Sepulchre
   (b) Knight of St John the Evangelist

STRUCTURE and QUALIFICATION

The office structure of a Conclave of the Red Cross of Constantine as shown below is quite different from those of a Sanctuary and Commandery of the Appendant Orders.

Red Cross of Constantine	Knights of the Holy Sepulchre and St John the Evangelist
Most Puissant Sovereign	Prelate
Viceroy	Commander
Senior General	Seneschal
Junior General	Captain of the Guards
High Prelate	Prior
Treasurer	Sub-Prior
Recorder	Treasurer
Almoner	Registrar
Marshal	Marshal
*Deputy Marshal	Deputy Marshal
Orator	First Lieutenant
Standard Bearer 'C'	Second Lieutenant
Standard Bearer 'L'	Guardian of the Sacred Vault
Prefect	Verger
*Assistant Recorder	Harbinger
*Organist	Torch Bearer
Senior Aide-de-camp	Standard Bearer
Junior Aide-de-camp	Warder
Herald	Sepulchre Guards (several)
*Stewards (3)	Beadle
Sentinel	—

Candidates after Installation are referred to as Worthy Knight Companions. The prerequisite qualification for membership of the Red Cross of Constantine is that of a Royal Arch Mason. All candidates for the Appendant Orders must have already been admitted as a Knight RCC.

REGALIA
Red Cross of Constantine: A Knight Companion of the Red Cross of Constantine traditionally wears a sash of purple silk four inches in width with gold tassels. The jewel of the Order is a Cross Flory in red enamel with gold edging and the initials IHSV; this is worn on the left breast suspended from a purple ribbon one inch in width. Swords are worn from the sash by Generals and Marshals.

Appendant Orders: Knights of the Holy Sepulchre and St John the Evangelist wear a sash of white watered silk four inches in width, having black tassels. Embroidered on the sash is a black eagle displayed looking backwards and walking to the left. Below this is the emblem of St John in silver which is a rayed triangle within an interlaced square and parallelogram all within a triple circle. Beneath the emblem are two black crosses Potent, one in the centre of the other bound by a black cord in the shape of a lozenge.

The jewel comprises a black eagle as on the sash, supporting a black lozenge bound by a looped gilt cord charged with two gilt crosses Potent one within the other. It is worn on the left breast suspended from a white ribbon one inch in width. Swords of the prescribed pattern are worn from the sash by the Captain of the Guards, the Lieutenants, the Marshals and the Sepulchre Guards.

Sovereigns and Past Sovereigns: Puissant Knights have a similar jewel to that of a Knight Companion in the Red Cross of Constantine, with the addition of the cross being surmounted by an imperial crown and charged with the Greek letters X and P. As a present or past Commander of the Appendant Orders, the breast jewel is a similar black eagle surmounted by a black

Left to right, Breast jewel of a commander of the Holy Sepulchre and St John the Evangelist, breast jewel of Knight Companion of Red Cross of Constantine, Grand Officer collarette and jewel (KHS), breast jewel for past Sovereign Red Cross of Constantine and breast jewel of a Knight of the Holy Sepulchre and St John the Evangelist.

imperial crown from which is suspended a black enamelled Jerusalem cross. In such instances a black embroidered imperial crown is situated above the eagle on the sash.

At the meeting of Grand Imperial Conclave in January 1981, amendments to the constitutions were promulgated whereby the Most Puissant Sovereign is further distinguished by a Red Cross Flory, surmounted by a gold imperial crown and charged with the letters X and P, which is worn from a collarette of white ribbon one inch in width.

Divisional Officers: The sash worn at divisional level is identical to that worn by a Knight Companion or Commander of the Appendant Orders, but is edged with crimson cord throughout, while the name of the division is embroidered in crimson in the form of an arc between the eagle and the emblem of St John.

Grand Officers: The jewel of this grade is an eagle surmounted by an imperial crown supporting a cross Potent, having a cross Flory diagonally across the angles, all in gilt and charged with a Jerusalem cross of black enamel. It is worn suspended from a two-inch wide collarette of white silk having a black border edged with gold braid. The sash is four inches wide, being white with a black and gold border, complete with tassels and bearing an imperial crown of crimson and gold, an eagle in gold, the emblem of St John in gold and a cross Potent as on the jewel in black. Intendants-General wear a robe of royal purple with gold coloured facings and carry a Sceptre of Office.

THE DEGREES
Knight of the Red Cross of Constantine: This degree relates the well-known story of Constantine the Great, the Roman Emperor who was miraculously converted to the Christian faith. It tells of his divine vision, the institution of a special standard, his subsequent victory over the rival Emperor Maxentius and the creation of what is claimed to be the oldest institution of Christian Knighthood. The substance of the degree develops around the secret doctrine associated with the Labarum, the banner of victory, while the lecture contains a

most interesting reference to the Roman College of Architects. All regular business of the Conclave is conducted in the degree of the Red Cross of Constantine, while the Sanctuary and Commandery are only for the purpose of conferring the Appendant Orders.

Knight of the Holy Sepulchre: Tradition asserts that this degree originated after the discovery of the true Cross by St Helena. It is concerned with the three days which intervened between the Crucifixion and the Resurrection. This Order of Chivalry is said to have been instituted by the mother of Constantine, to maintain a guard at the Holy Place and is symbolised in the ceremony by a vigil over the HS. The duties enjoined on the Knights were the performance of the seven works of mercy.

Knight of St John the Evangelist: This is the second of the Appendant degrees which are always conferred together and is founded upon a tradition concerning a remarkable discovery made at the ruins of the Temple at Jerusalem and the subsequent foundation of the Knights of St John. The interpretation of the legend is of a most interesting and instructive nature and is striking in its attempt to explain the Craft and Royal Arch ceremonies in a purely Christian sense.

Knights Templar and Knights of Malta

The full title of this Order is—The United Religious, Military and Masonic Orders of the Temple and of St John of Jerusalem, Palestine, Rhodes and Malta, in England and Wales and Provinces Overseas. The Orders are governed by a Great Priory.

HISTORY and ORIGIN
In considering this impressive title and the joining together of two Orders who were at one time, while not actual enemies, militant rivals, one must really appreciate that no claim is made to any historical connection with the medieval Military Orders. Whilst the earliest references to Masonic Knight Templar activity in the British Isles are to be found in Ireland, the earliest known records in England were minuted at Portsmouth in 1777. In most instances these rituals appear to have been worked under the authority of existing warrants of certain Royal Arch Chapters as appendant degrees and were not organised masonically in any strict sense of the word. It was not until 1791 that a Grand Conclave was formed comprising seven independent Encampments, when Thomas Dunckerley was installed as Grand Master.

Expansion during the formative years was extremely slow, particularly under the Grand Mastership of HRH the Duke of Sussex (1812–1843) who displayed no desire to convene Grand Conclave and consequently there was little activity until after his death. The reason for this inactivity was probably due to the delicate state of affairs in freemasonry immediately following the Union. From 1845 onwards, however, conditions within the Order were restored to normal; the ritual was standardised and a steady growth of the United Orders ensued and today membership is by invitation and highly valued. The degrees as practised in over 490 Preceptories on the roll of the Great Priory of England are:

1. Knight of the Temple (Knight Templar)
2. (a) Knight of St Paul or Mediterranean Pass
   (b) Knight of Malta

STRUCTURE and QUALIFICATION

The assemblies of Knights Templar are described as Preceptories, and under the authority of its warrant a Preceptory has power to hold a Priory of Knights of Malta. A candidate for Installation into Knighthood must be of the Christian faith, a Master Mason and a Royal Arch Mason. The officers of a Preceptory and Priory are:

Knights Templar	Knights of Malta
Eminent Preceptor	Eminent Prior
Chaplain	Captain General
First Constable	Lieutenant General
Second Constable	First Lieutenant
Treasurer	Second Lieutenant
Registrar	Chaplain
Marshal	Mareschal
*Deputy Marshal	Deputy Mareschal
*Almoner	Hospitaller
*First Herald	Admiral
*Second Herald	Conservator
*First Standard Bearer	Baillie
*Second Standard Bearer	Turcopolier
Captain of Guards	Chancellor
*Organist	Treasurer
*Stewards	Captain of Outposts
Guard	Guard

Every candidate for the Order of Malta must have first been received into the Order of the Temple.

REGALIA

Knight Templar: The regalia of this Order is most impressive, being based on the costume of the medieval counterparts and comprises a mantle, tunic, cap, sash, cross, star, belt and sword.

The mantle is of white material having a hood with silken tasselled cords and lining and a red Cross Pateé fixed below the left shoulder. The tunic is of matching material being at least knee length with a Latin cross in red the full length of the front. The cap is of red velvet, three inches deep with a silver Cross Pateé at the front. The sash is black watered silk, four inches wide with a silver knot and black silk fringe. The cross

Top, left to right, Breast jewel worn by members of Knights of Malta, Past Preceptor's collarette jewel, Cross Pateé breast jewel worn by members of Knights Templar. Bottom row shows the star jewels for Preceptor (left) and Knights (right).

of a Knight is a red enamelled gilt Cross Pateé worn on the left breast suspended from a red ribbon with white edging. The star is seven-pointed of silver metal in the centre of which is a Passion cross of red enamel on a white background girded with a black garter bearing the inscription 'In Hoc Signo Vinces'.

The sword should be of straight pattern with a straight cross hilt and is usually worn from a leather thonged belt. Black gloves or gauntlets are also worn.

Preceptors and Priors: Holders of this rank wear identical regalia to a knight of the Order with the following changes. The mantle hood is changed to red lining as is the cord and tassels; a patriarchal cross (the lower arm wider than the upper) is worn on the mantle below the left shoulder; the cap badge is changed to a patriarchal cross as is the centre of the star jewel. A Preceptor will wear a red enamel patriarchal cross from a neck ribbon in the colours of the Order while Past Preceptors wear a jewel of special design.

Provincial Officers: The minor differences in regalia worn by provincial officers is that a badge designating the office held is worn on the mantle cross. This badge takes the form of the emblem of office surrounded by a garter in dark blue. The black sash has the addition of a half-inch white stripe running down the centre.

Great Officers: The major difference to that of the normal regalia is that the badge of office is worn superimposed on the mantle cross; the patriarchal cross on the cap is changed to gold colour and the black sash has three white stripes and a gold fringe.

Knight of Malta: The regalia of the Order is composed of a mantle, tunic, cap, cross jewel, belt and sword.

The mantle is of black material with tassels and the hood lining in white. A white Maltese cross 14 inches across is worn below the left shoulder. The tunic is of red material, knee length, with a similar Maltese cross on the centre of the breast. The cap is black velvet with a white enamelled Maltese cross of metal gilt on the front. The jewel is a Maltese cross, being gilt with lions of silver between the arms; it is worn on the left breast suspended by a silver bow from a black ribbon. Similar gloves, belt and sword to those in the Templar grade are worn. While the regalia for the Malta degree is listed in the statutes it is permissible for Templar regalia to be worn.

Priors wear a crowned Maltese cross having lions of gold between the arms of the cross and the whole is suspended from the neck by a black ribbon. Past Priors wear the collarette and composite jewel of a Past Preceptor/Prior from a red and white ribbon, one and three-quarter inches wide. Great Officers wear a jewel depicting the Maltese cross complete with lions which is girded by a garter in black enamel and suspended from a black and white collarette.

THE DEGREES

Knight Templar: This degree commemorates the actions of a band of knights who were granted a place of habitation within the sacred precincts of KST by Baldwin II King of Jerusalem in 1118. A candidate for installation is admitted in the character and garb of a pilgrim and is required to undergo a period of pilgrimage and warfare as well as to assume the vows of a crusader. Having conducted himself courageously, he is then instructed how penance and meditation play their vital part in preparation for Christian knighthood and finally he is received, armed and proclaimed a Knight of the Temple. It is in this degree that all general business of the Preceptory is carried out.

Knight of St Paul or Mediterranean Pass: The ritual of this small 'passing' degree informs us that it was founded around the year 1367 in consequence of a certain battle involving the Knights of St John of Rhodes, when crossing the River Offanto which was reputedly stained with the blood of their vanquished enemies. Through the ensuing victory the knights secured recognition to pass and repass all parts of the Mediterranean coastline without molestation. The degree, however, as now worked is confined to scriptural readings from *The Acts* of the Apostles.

Knight of St John of Jerusalem, Palestine, Rhodes and Malta: This degree of Christian Knighthood recounts the history of the Knights of Malta and their long struggle against the infidel. It traces their progress from the time they left Jerusalem until they reached their final home on the island of Malta. The attention of all candidates is drawn to the presence of five officers who assume the role of personal staff of the Grand Master, while the other officers represent the heads of the eight Langues or Tongues, into which the ancient Order was divided. The ritual has an obvious esoteric meaning, being one of mystical resurrection.

Holy Royal Arch Knight Templar Priests

HISTORY and ORIGIN

It appears that this degree has its foundation in Ireland where records exist of workings in the late 1700s. It is reasonably asserted that in early days, Knights Templar from various Craft lodges joined together as a 'Union Band' for the purpose of conferring the degree, but there appears to have been no governing body to exercise control and guidance, which must have contributed in no small measure to its chequered existence. In 1895 a Tabernacle (The Royal Kent) was created at Newcastle-upon-Tyne and, while the Order of Knight Templar Priests and its appendant orders were for a time taken under the jurisdiction of the Grand Council of Allied Masonic Degrees, the Royal Kent Tabernacle continued to confer the degree. In 1923 the present Grand College was formed at Newcastle and from that time there has been continued healthy expansion of the Order. There are now in excess of 180 Tabernacles owing allegiance to this sovereign body, spread not only throughout England, but also in Australia, New Zealand, Hong Kong, Canada and South Africa. The degrees controlled are:

Funeral Master
Master of the Blue or
    Knight of Solomon
Most Excellent Master
Excellent Mason and
    Master of the Veils
Sublime Master or
    Jacob's Wrestle

Fugitive Mark
Architect
Order of the Scarlet Cord or
    Knight of Rahab
Knight of the Three Kings or
    The Balance
Knight of the North
Knight of the South

Knight of Patmos or Philippi
Knight of Redemption
Knight of Death or Elysium
Knight of the Holy Grave
Knight of the Christian Mark
Knight of Bethany
Knight of the Royal Prussian Blue
Knight of Eleusis
Knight of Palestine
Knight of Saint John the Baptist
Knight of the Cross
Knight of the Black Cross

Knight of the White Cross
Knight of the White of Cross Torphichen
Knight of the Suspended Cross of Babylon
Knight of the Red Cross of Jerusalem
Knight of the Red Cross or Roseae Crucis
Knight of the Triple Cross
Grand Cross of Saint John
Made free from Harodim
Holy Royal Arch Knight Templar Priest

STRUCTURE and QUALIFICATION

Gatherings of this order are described as Tabernacles and members are referred to as Knight Priests. The office structure is as follows:

High Priest
VIIth Pillar
VIth Pillar
Treasurer
Recorder
Director of Ceremonies
Vth Pillar
IVth Pillar
IIIrd Pillar

IInd Pillar
Ist Pillar
Conductor
*Assistant Director of Ceremonies
*Organist
Keeper of the Inner Porch
*Steward
Outer Sentinel

The prerequisite qualifications for this order are threefold and demand that a candidate shall be:

    (a) an Installed Master in the Craft;

    (b) a Royal Arch Mason; and

    (c) a Knight Templar

Tabernacles of the Order are grouped into Districts under the control of a Grand Inspector.

REGALIA

The clothing of the Order consists of a white tunic having a full length cross of red to the front, over which is worn a white mantle (it is permissible for the Knight Templar mantle and tunic to be worn). A mitre is also worn by Knight Priests which is required to be eight inches high and having a red cross in front, while that of a High Priest (and Past High Priests) is 12 inches in height and features a Patriarchal cross (cross with two bars).

Grand College Officers: Past and Present officers of Grand College wear an identical mitre to that of a Past High Priest with the addition of gold embroidered croziers crossed at the intersection of the bottom arm of the cross, on which is superimposed the number of their pillar or the initials of their respective rank. In the case of a Grand Steward the symbol of a gilt Cornucopia is affixed, while the Grand Superintendent of a Division has the initials GS.

THE DEGREES

As can be seen, Grand College has right over in excess of 30 degrees, but most are conferred on the candidate 'by name'; it is the final degree only which is worked in full, that of Holy Royal Arch Knight Templar Priest. The ceremony consists in the main of readings from the Old and New Testaments. The candidate is conducted to seven pillars, placed in the form of a triangle, at each of which is stationed a Pillar Officer. Each pillar has a word referring to the attributes of the Lamb of God who opened the seven seals, revealing the various Spirits of God. The symbol of the Order is an equilateral triangle upon which are inscribed certain important letters alluding to the secrets of the degree.

Royal Order of Scotland

HISTORY and ORIGIN

Authentic documentary proof in the archives of the Grand Lodge gives rise to the popular assertion that the Royal Order of Scotland is senior to every other masonic system, with the exception of the Craft, for there is written and printed evidence that a number of Lodges of the Order were active in London as early as in 1741. A zealous mason by the name of William Mitchell, then living in the Low Countries, applied to the authorities in London in 1750 for a charter to hold a Lodge of the Order at The Hague, and while this charter was granted it is doubtful if the Lodge ever worked. About 1752 or 1753 Brother Mitchell moved to Edinburgh taking with him the Charter issued to him as Provincial Grand Master at The Hague and by virtue of this document he set up a Lodge of the Royal Order in Edinburgh; in due course this body was to elevate itself to the rank of Grand Lodge of the Royal Order of Scotland in July 1767. A period transpired in the early 1800s when the Order nearly became extinct for few meetings were held, but in 1839 efforts at resuscitation were successful and by 1843 Grand Lodge was granting warrants for the erection of Provincial Grand Lodges.

From the earliest written records of meetings, the Order claimed that the King of Scots was the Hereditary Grand Master and a seat in the East is kept vacant for him at every meeting of each Provincial Grand Lodge, and at all meetings of Grand Lodge.

The Grand Lodge at Edinburgh today controls some 85 Provincial Grand Lodges situated in many different parts of the world. The Royal Order of Scotland contains two degrees, namely:

1. The Heredom of Kilwinning
2. Knighthood of the Rosy Cross

Understandably, membership of this elite order is highly prized, admission to the Order being by invitation only.

STRUCTURE and QUALIFICATION

With regular bodies of the Order enjoying the status of a Provincial Grand Lodge, it naturally follows that the immediate authority is vested in a Provincial Grand Master who is supported by a team of officers as follows:

Deputy Provincial Grand Master
Substitute Provincial Grand Master
Senior Provincial Grand Warden
Junior Provincial Grand Warden
Provincial Grand Treasurer
Provincial Grand Secretary
Provincial Grand Chaplain
Provincial Grand Sword Bearer
Provincial Grand Banner Bearer
Provincial Grand Marischal
Deputy Provincial Grand Marischal
Provincial Grand Introductor & Examiner
Provincial Grand Constable of the Tower
First Provincial Grand Steward
Second Provincial Grand Steward
Provincial Grand Director of Music
Provincial Grand Guarder
Deputy Provincial Grand Guarder

Qualifications as laid down, demand that prospective candidates must be Master Masons of at least five years' standing, although other specific conditions of entry are often insisted upon.

REGALIA

A brother on reception into the first degree is clothed with an apron of special design, 14 inches wide at the top and 15½ inches

Regalia worn by members of the Royal Order of Scotland.

wide at the bottom. It is of white lambskin edged with crimson ribbon and having a triangular flap with a matching fringe. He is also invested with a crimson cordon or baldrick four inches wide which is worn over the left shoulder and under the right arm. On promotion to the second degree, the former apron is replaced by one of similar dimensions, but edged with crimson and thistle green ribbon, and having a fringed flap of green. An identical cordon of green is worn over that of crimson, from the right shoulder and under the left arm. On the left breast, a seven-pointed gilt star is worn, featuring the cross of the Order in the centre. A garter of thistle green edged with gold, bearing the words 'Virtute et Silentio' is normally worn round the left arm, but when wearing the kilt it is placed around the left leg, below the knee. The regalia of Grand Officers with minor exceptions is that worn by their counterparts within a Provincial Grand Lodge.

THE DEGREES
The Heredom of Kilwinning: According to tradition this degree originated during the reign of David I in the twelfth century and is noticeably Christian in character, depicting freemasonry in a purely Christian aspect. Most of the ritual is couched in quaint old doggerel verse and is worked mainly by question and answer, as in the Craft lectures, but embracing elements and references found in many other degrees. Choice of a characteristic, typical of some moral attribute or virtue, is one of the peculiarities of the Order, this being spelt without the use of vowels. Armed with his particular characteristic, the candidate is sent forth in search of the lost word.

Knight of the Rosy Cross: This degree of Knighthood is said to have been instituted by King Robert the Bruce immediately after the Battle of Bannockburn in 1314, to commemorate the valour of a band of knights and masons who had signally aided him in the great victory. He revived the older degree and incorporated the two under the title of the Royal Order of Scotland and traditionally he established the chief seat of the order at Kilwinning. This degree traces its course from the Old to the New Testament and finally culminates with the secret doctrine inculcated in the life and death of our Saviour. It is asserted by many that the RSYCS contains the ceremonial of admission formerly practised in the most ancient Order of the Thistle.

The Rite of Baldwyn of Seven Degrees TI at Bristol

This series of degrees, termed the Baldwyn Rite, is a unique survival of speculative ceremonies which constitute the Rite of Seven Degrees with Time Immemorial status, centred at Bristol. The earliest record relating to the Baldwyn Encampment is a curious document known as the Charter of Compact which was drawn up in 1780, containing rules for regulating the erection of a Supreme Grand and Royal Encampment. In 1791 Thomas Dunckerley, who was Provincial Grand Master for Bristol for seven years and also Grand Master of the Templars, issued a Patent of Constitution (Warrant) empowering certain brethren to hold 'a Conclave of Encampment at the City of Bristol of the Seven Degrees of Time Immemorial'.

In 1843, following the death of the Duke of Sussex, the Grand Conclave of England (the Templars) was revived and the degree of Rose Croix was passed to the jurisdiction of the Supreme Council 33°. Very soon after the Bristol brethren were invited to submit to the authority of the two Grand bodies, but they were concerned for the welfare of their Rite and gracefully declined. A period of negotiation then took place and in May 1862 a Charter of Compact was drawn up with the Grand Conclave of England, constituting Bristol as a Provincial Commandery (the Provincial Priory of today) being Time Immemorial and allowed to continue its own working of the Hospitaller and Templar grades. It was a further 19 years, however, before a Treaty of Union was entered into with the Supreme Council 33°, constituting Bristol as a

OFFICE STRUCTURE of The Camp of Baldwyn

III°
Knights of the Nine Elected Masters

Most Potent Commander
Constable
Master of Ceremonies
First Captain
Second Captain
Recorder
Herald
Standard Bearer
Inner Equerry
KS
KH

IV°
Scots Knights Grand Architect
(In Scots dress)

Most Potent Commander
High Priest
Recorder & Compthier
Master of Ceremonies
First Captain
Second Captain
Inner Equerry
Herald
First Standard Bearer
Second Standard Bearer

Scots Knights of Kilwinning*
(In Templar dress)

Eminent Commander & Preceptor
Past Emt Cmdr & Preceptor
Prelate
Marshal
First Constable
Second Constable
Captain of the Guard
* By tradition the ceremony of
this Templar Order follows that
of the IV°

V°
Knights of the East, the Sword and Eagle

Most Potent Commander
First General
Second General
Master of Ceremonies
Recorder
Asst Master of Ceremonies
First Guard
Second Guard
Herald
Standard Bearer

VI°
Knights of St John and Knights Templar

Part two

First Principal
Second Principal
Third Principal
Scribe E
Scribe N

Emt Comm and Preceptor
Prelate
First Constable
Second Constable
Treasurer
Registrar
Marshal
Sub-Marshal
Captain of Guard
Herald
First Standard Bearer
Second Standard Bearer

VII°
Knights of the Rose Croix

Most Wise Sovereign
Prelate
First General
Second General
Treasurer
Recorder
Raphael
Master of Ceremonies
Asst. Master of Ceremonies
Inner Equerry
First Standard Bearer
Second Standard Bearer
Herald

District TI with an Inspector General and its own version of the Rose Croix degree. The composition of the Rite is as follows:

I°   Craft
II°   The Supreme Order of the Holy Royal Arch

THE CAMP OF BALDWYN
(The Five Royal Orders of Knighthood)

III°   Knights of the Nine Elected Masters
IV°   The Ancient Order of Scots Knights Grand Architect (traditionally followed by the Royal Order of Scots Knights of Kilwinning)
V°   Knights of the East, The Sword and Eagle
VI°   Knights of St John of Jerusalem, Palestine, Rhodes and Malta, and Knights Templar
VII°   Knights of the Rose Croix of Mount Carmel

STRUCTURE and QUALIFICATION

The office structure of the five Royal Orders of Knighthood within the Baldwyn Rite is shown on the accompanying chart. As it has always been considered important to maintain their valued traditions, it is essential that the Provincial Prior (VI°), the Grand Inspector General (VII°) and the Grand Superintendent of the Rite of Baldwyn, be one and the same person.

While admissions are strictly by invitation, certain unusual qualifications pertain here as a candidate is not eligible for reception into the Camp of Baldwyn without having previously been exalted in a Bristol Chapter of the Royal Arch. A further condition prevails in admission to the degree of Rose Croix; this not being permissible unless the candidate is already in possession of their Templar grade.

REGALIA

There are special jewels worn by the Most Potent Commanders in the III°, IV°, and V° degrees, while the regalia of the VI° and VII° degrees are generally identical to those worn in the Knights Templar and Rose Croix. In addition, there is a

*The special breast jewel peculiar to
members of the Baldwyn Rite.*

special breast jewel peculiar to members of the Baldwyn Rite;
it comprises of a Maltese cross of silver having eight points
and in its centre a seven-pointed star bearing the initials ETH,
while the reverse features a twin-headed eagle in its centre.
The cross is suspended from a silver bar by a black ribbon one
inch wide having a white stripe each side. These jewels are of a
very special nature as they are invariably made of hand
engraved silver.

The Grand Superintendent wears a collarette in the black
and white ribbon of the Rite, from which is suspended a
Greek cross of special design superimposed upon a 12-pointed
star (eight arms exposed) and bears the initials E—SHEH.

By the terms of the Treaty of Union (1881) Baldwyn

Chapter Rose Croix still wear the full regalia of apron, gilt-handled sword with red scabbard and belt, and white gloves in members' own chapter.

THE DEGREES

I° The Craft: Consists of the three established degrees of the Craft which may be acquired in any regular lodge.

II° The Supreme Order of the Holy Royal Arch: This grade must be received through a Bristol Chapter where this degree incorporates the ceremony of 'Passing of the Veils', which is said to correspond with the various spiritual states of existence which lie beyond the grave.

THE CAMP OF BALDWYN

III° Knights of the Nine Elected Masters: This degree was resuscitated in November 1934 when the ceremony was worked in full.

IV° Scots Knights Grand Architect and Scots Knights of Kilwinning: A full revival of this Templar degree was accomplished in September 1921 and subsequently many distinguished brethren from outside were received into this degree (a practice which has long since ceased). This degree is strongly Templar in tone.

V° Knights of the East, the Sword and Eagle: This degree was also revived in full in November 1934.

The III°, IV° and V° degrees are believed to have been introduced from France about 1813 and appear to have been possibly connected with the 'Rit Moderne', but it is not known when they first became established in Bristol. While they were not revived in full until the twentieth century, successive Superintendents of the Rite have ensured that the essentials of these three degrees have never been allowed to lapse and today they are performed in their entirety, at regular intervals.

VI° Knights of St John of Jerusalem, Palestine, Rhodes and Malta, and Knights Templar. As can be envisaged from the title of the sixth degree of the Rite, the Hospitaller's part is decidedly more prominent than that of the Templar; another unusual feature is the practice of conferring the grades of Malta and the Temple in one ceremony.

VII° Knights of the Rose Croix of Mount Carmel: The *ne plus ultra* of the Baldwyn Rite.

Nominally the proper sequence of degrees is as listed above, but in practice it is not always practical or possible to follow it. Candidates are received into the Camp through Installation as Knights of the Hospital and Temple and as such present themselves for Perfection in the Rose Croix Chapter; before attaining this, however, they are entrusted with the passwords of the other degrees (ie III, IV and V).

The Operatives

The full title of this Order is the Worshipful Society of Free Masons, Rough Masons, Walkers, Slaters, Paviours, Plaisterer's and Bricklayers.

HISTORY and ORIGIN

The constitutions of the Society state that the Order was founded in 1913, although claims of certain members (circa 1910) hinted at a much more ancient vintage. A paper by W Bro Thomas Carr published in the 1911–12 *Transactions of the Leicester Lodge of Research No 2429* explained much of the ceremonial working of the 'Operative' Lodge. In due course on 21 May 1913, the Channel Row Assemblage was reconstituted (?) at Bedford House, just off the Strand, when W Bro Carr officiated as Enthroning Master under a special letter of authority, issued by 'the Masters' and signed by the Secretary of the York Division (W Bro Clement E. Stretton). The ritual of 'the Operatives' as they are familiarly called, is more archaic in form and much fuller than that of 'the Speculatives', containing practical instruction of which only echoes are found in speculative ritual, thereby providing an interesting field of study for the serious masonic student. The degrees of the Society are seven in number, namely:

I°	Indentured Apprentice
II°	Fellow of the Craft
III°	Super-Fellow, Fitter & Marker
IV°	Super-Fellow, Setter Erector
V°	Intendent, Overseer, Superintendant & Warden
VI°	Passed Master
VII°	Passed Grand Master Mason

There are at present some 35 Assemblages of the Society and its unique character is gaining interest in Masonic circles throughout England and abroad.

STRUCTURE and QUALIFICATION

Bodies are termed as Assemblages, consisting of one Lodge of each Degree, from Fourth to First, which is ruled by a Deputy Master Mason, who as Senior Passed Master is the local representative of the (three) Grand Master Masons. The officers of an Assemblage IV°–I° are as follows:

> Deputy Master Mason
> Deputy J (Chaplain)
> Deputy B
> Superintendant of Works
> Senior Warden
> Junior Warden
> Treasurer
> Clerk (Secretary)
> Deputy Master Mason's Deacon
> Senior Warden's Deacon
> Junior Warden's Deacon
> *Deputy Superintendant of Works
> *Orator
> *Organist
> Inside Guard
> *Stewards
> Outside Guard

Lodges of the V° and VI° function under the auspices of the Grand Assemblage and are controlled by a duly authorised Deputy Master Mason appointed by the Grand Master Masons, while the VII° degree Lodge is under their direct control.

Membership is limited to candidates who must be a Master Mason, a Mark Master Mason and a Royal Arch Companion in good standing. Once accepted, a candidate can progress to the V° without additional qualification, but he must be an Installed Master in both Craft and Mark before he can be raised to the VI°.

Operatives III jewel.

REGALIA

I° On admission to the Society an 'Indentured Apprentice' is invested with a thin pale blue cord.

II° As a 'Fellow of the Craft', he is presented with a 'Square Guage' of bronze which is suspended from the pale blue cord.

III° The jewel of a 'Fitter and Marker' is a 'Running Stone Guage' in bronze which is again suspended from the cord.

IV° On advancement to 'Setter Erector' the recipient acquires a jewel in bronze of a 'Footing Corner Stone Guage' which is affixed to the cord.

V° A one-inch collar of pale blue ribbon replaces the cord for an 'Intendent and Superintendant' and an 'Elbow Square Guage' of silver is suspended therefrom.

VI° On becoming a 'Passed Master' the previous jewel is replaced by a silver square.

VII° In the final degree of 'Passed Grand Master' a golden square is worn from the one-inch pale blue collarette.

In addition to the above insignia which indicates the degree held by the wearer, each Assemblage provides for its officers jewels, which are worn on a pale blue collarette two inches in width.

THE DEGREES

I° **Indentured Apprentice:** On applying for admission, a candidate must complete a petition stating that he is a free man and of full years; he then pays a Footing Fee and is duly obligated on the Rough Ashlar and bound by the oath of Nimrod. After submitting a test of his skill he is eligible to be made 'free of his bonds' and passed to the degree of . . .

II° **Fellow of the Craft:** His bonds of indenture are cancelled and he is set to work in the second stoneyard where he is taught to render his ashlar true and polished. After inspection of his work he is instructed in the traditional history and given an unusual explanation of the working tools. He is then enabled to progress to the third degree of . . . .

III° **Super-Fellow, Fitter and Marker:** This degree has a near affinity with that of Mark Man and he is enjoined to produce 'fair work and square' when producing stones for the building. After the requisite period he may apply to be advanced to . . .

IV° **Super-Fellow, Setter Erector:** Here the candidate is entitled by qualification to work on site in a ceremony that embodies practical emphasis as applied to the speculative degree of Mark Master. He is erected as a Living Stone and duly signs the roll; in due time he is considered for admission to the grade of . . .

V° Intendent, Overseer, Superintendant and Warden: Acceptance into a Lodge of Menatzchim has no exact correspondence in speculative masonry, for here every candidate is examined as to his technical knowledge before being obligated as an Overseer within the Society, after which he is charged to apply his mark with strict caution. Further progress is now conditional on the brother having served in the chair of KS as well as that of A before he can hope to be raised as a . . .

VI° Passed Master: It is only on admission to a Lodge of Harodim that a brother can assume a senior role within an Assemblage. The raising in this degree must not be confused with that of a speculative lodge, for here it has a truly operative connotation. He must understand his profession thoroughly before he can be received and become a representation of the perfect corner stone. It is only after long service in the Society that a member may be exalted to the supreme grade where he assumes the title of . . .

VII° Passed Grand Master Mason: There are only three Grand Master Masons in practice, the first (SKI) and second (HKT) traditionally holding office for life, while the third is ritually slain in October of every year, when a new grand master is enthroned in his place following the 'Enactment of the Drama'. Other brethren are from time to time exalted to this degree, when the esoteric teaching in relation to the symbol of the Society and the secret tradition of the 3, 4, 5 triangle and the real seat of the power of the Most High is revealed to them.

Societas Rosicruciana in Anglia

(The Rosicrucian Society of Freemasons)

HISTORY and ORIGIN

The modern society of Rosicrucians was given its present form by Robert Wentworth Little in 1865, who with other zealous masons founded the order following the reputed discovery of certain manuscripts in the archives of Grand Lodge. The society was based upon symbolism and traditions of a much earlier Society known as the Fraternity of the Rose and Cross, which in turn claimed its origin from an immortal character, real or mythical, known as Christian Rosenkreutz and familiarly designated by the initials CRC. This society subsequently gave rise to other bodies in Scotland and the USA, and in building upon the ancient order the modern societies have not departed from precedent, but have continued the eternal search for knowledge. This is evinced by the encouragement given for members to produce papers and deliver lectures as a vital part of College work. The Society has power to confer nine grades as follows:

I°	Zelator
II°	Theoricus
III°	Practicus
IV°	Philosophus
V°	Adeptus Minor
VI°	Adeptus Major
VII°	Adeptus Exemptus
VIII°	Magister
IX°	Magus

There are 58 Colleges in the English Society, spread as far afield as Australia, Canada and New Zealand.

STRUCTURE and QUALIFICATION

Assemblies of the Society are termed Colleges and are grouped into Provinces under Chief Adepts and their Suffragans. Officers are,

Celebrant	*Precentor
Exponent	*Organist
*Chaplain	*Assistant Secretary
Treasurer	*Librarian
Secretary	*Registrar of Mottoes
*Director of Ceremonies	Herald
Ancients (four)	Guardian
Conductor of Novices	*Cellarius (3)
Torch Bearer	Acolyte

It is normal for the Chief Adept or his Suffragan in the absence of the Supreme Magus, to install the Celebrant of each College in his Province, although he may appoint some other duly qualified Magister to act for him. The Celebrant in every case must before installation, have received the Grade of Adeptus Exemptus and have duly served the office of Exponent of a College. Members are recognised as Fratres. All candidates are required to be Master Masons subscribing to a regular lodge on the register of the Grand Lodge of England or a Grand Lodge in amity therewith. They must be of high moral character and fully embrace the principles of Christianity; it is expected that they will be of sufficient ability to appreciate the studies of the Society, which consider the revelation of philosophy, science and theosophy.

REGALIA

All members of the Society are required to wear the jewel of their grade as follows:

I–IV Grades: These wear a white enamelled gilt metal lozenge bearing a red cross with arms of equal length, suspended from

SRIA breast jewel worn by members of the I-IV Grades.

a green silk ribbon attached to a gilt bar bearing the initials SRIA.

V–VII Grades: Members wear an identical jewel to the first four grades suspended from a yellow silk ribbon with the respective Roman numerals embroidered in violet silk.

VIII Grade: As a Magister (Honoris Causa 8°) the standard pattern lozenge of white and red is worn surmounted by a golden mitre bearing the word LUX suspended from a red silk ribbon. A Magister High Councillor VIII° wears the same jewel suspended from a red silk collarette.

IX Grade: As a Magus (Honoris Causa 9°) a black Calvary cross, having a small rose of silver on each arm and a miniature lozenge of the Society in the centre, is worn suspended from a red silk ribbon. The Supreme Magus and Substitute Magi IX°, wear larger crosses of similar pattern suspended from red velvet collarettes.

In addition the Officers of a College are furnished with a robe of office, depicting by colour or emblem their particular function.

Celebrant: The Celebrant of a College wears a surplice shaped robe of crimson bearing a white cross of four equal arms on the left breast, together with a red silk collarette from which is suspended the white enamelled lozenge of the order, surmounted by a celestial crown. A Past Celebrant wears a similar crimson robe on which the cross is surrounded by a white lozenge edging, while he has a white enamelled lozenge suspended from a red ribbon on the left breast. When a Celebrant or Past Celebrant is a Magister (8° or VIII°) the emblem on the robe is surmounted by a mitre of white.

Provincial Officers: The Chief Adept of a Province wears a hooded robe of crimson, which has a Calvary cross with a mitre above it embroidered in gold on the left breast. He also wears a standard pattern lozenge of the Society, gold in colour and surmounted by a similar coloured mitre, suspended from a red silk collarette. His Suffragan (Deputy) wears a similar robe with the symbols in white, while the golden collarette jewel is without the mitre. Provincial Officers may also wear the same jewel as a Suffragan, but do not have any special robe.

High Councillors: A High Councillor VII° wears a robe of crimson edged with blue silk, bearing a cross with arms of equal length embroidered in gold on the left breast, together with a gold triangular plate bearing a red enamelled cross in the centre, suspended from a yellow (Adepts colour) collarette. A Magister High Councillor VIII° has a similar robe, with the addition of a mitre in gold and he wears the collarette specified above. (See VIII Grade.)

Officers of High Council, with the exception of the Magi, wear crimson robes edged with various colours pertinent to their office, together with an appropriate embroidered symbol on the left breast. The Magi wear robes of red velvet.

THE GRADES

Of the nine grades, four are grouped in the 'First Order' and may be conferred by a Celebrant of a College in open Temple.

I° **Zelator:** This is the first grade of the Society, where the aspirant is received in a most impressive and colourful ceremony and where he is exhorted to commence his quest for true wisdom. All business of the College is transacted in this grade.

II° **Theoricus:** As implied by the title, the ritual of admission is concerned with the theoretical aspects of divinity in all its forms. This grade embodies an erudite lecture on colour.

III° **Practicus:** The study and ritual of this grade has special reference to the spiritual facet of the ancient art of alchemy.

IV° **Philosophus:** Here the aspirant is encouraged to expand his knowledge by careful study of the various philosophical and sacred writings of the World religions. An extensive lecture of superb calibre is embodied within this grade.

The 'Second Order' comprises of the Vth–VIIth grades, variously known as the Adept Grades which are conferred in a College of Adepts by a Chief Adept or his duly appointed deputy. Selection for advancement in the Adept grades is made by the Supreme Magus or Chief Adept only.

V° **Adeptus Minor:** Admission to this grade is not permissible until a minimum period of four years has been served in the Society. This is a pre-requisite grade for advancement to the office of Ancient within a College.

VI° **Adeptus Major:** The sixth grade is one with great significance and demands a high degree of contemplation in preparation for advancement to the seventh grade of . . .

VII° **Adeptus Exemptus:** This, the final grade of the 'Second Order', is pre-requisite for installation into the chair of a College. The teachings embodied are of a divine and ethereal nature, designed to elevate the mind in preparation for complete initiation.

The Third Order: The two grades are conferred by the Supreme Magus, or by special dispensation by another Magus.

Selection for these grades is made by the Supreme Magus only, the third being the ruling Order of the Society.

VIII° Magister: This grade is conferred upon the Officers of the High Council designated in the Ordinances of the Society and may be conferred upon other members of the High Council. 8° Magister (Honoris Causa) may be conferred upon other Fratres who show outstanding service to the Society. A Magister High Councillor on ceasing to be a member of the High Council reverts to the rank of Magister (Honoris Causa) 8°.

IX° Magus: This rank is only held by the Supreme Magus, the Senior Substitute Magus and the Junior Substitute Magus. The rank of Magus (Honoris Causa) 9° may be conferred by the Supreme Magus on a Frater who has shown outstanding devotion to the aims of the Society and there are but few Fraters who attain it.

The Electoral College is composed of all members of the Third Order who are subscribing members of a College of the Society and is responsible for the election of a new Supreme Magus when that Office falls vacant.

The August Order of Light

HISTORY and ORIGIN

This Oriental Order is founded upon the literature supplied by a Dr Maurice Vidal Portman, a learned student of Oriental lore, an occultist, freemason and politician who spent a considerable time on the staff of the Diplomatic Corps in India and the Andaman Islands during the late 1800s. He made himself familiar with the literature and ritual observances of the Eastern Indian races, whether Brahmins, Buddhists, Jains or Mohammedans, and gained much curious lore from religious devotees of all creeds. He also studied many quaint traditions and magical arts of learned natives throughout Asia and the Middle East. The Order in its first form was not widely known and for some years was in abeyance, but in time Bro T. H. Pattison and Bro B. E. J. Edwards were chosen (because of their extensive study of Oriental literature) to recast the original material into a series of degrees. Consequently in 1902 Bro Pattison became the first Guardian of Light, he being succeeded by Bro Edwards in the following year and in token of their pre-eminence they became the first Arch Presidents of the Centre. The degrees as now worked are as follows:

1. First Degree
2. Passing Degree
3. Second Degree

The Garuda Temple No 1 as it is called was centred at Bradford, where for many years an elaborate chamber was maintained especially for the Order, but in recent times it was found necessary to relocate the Temple firstly to York and recently in Halifax. With the increasing popularity of the Order a further Temple (The Garuda Temple No 2) was founded in London in 1970.

STRUCTURE and QUALIFICATION
Regular bodies of the Order are known as Temples and meetings are referred to as Ashayana. The officers of the Chakram are as follows:

First Degree	Passing Degree	Second Degree
Guardian of Light	President of Garuda	Indra
Guardian of the West	Guardian of the West	Guardian of the West
Guardian of the South	Guardian of the South	Guardian of the South
Aruna	Aruna	Aruna
Yama	Yama	Yama
Kuvera	Kuvera	Kuvera
Durwan	Durwan	Durwan
		Akasha
		Vayu
		Agni
		Apas
		Prithwi

Membership is open to invited Master Masons, but an important prerequisite is that an intending candidate is required to present a paper before his application can be considered. The subject of the paper may be of his choosing, but may not be of a political or masonic nature.

REGALIA
In this series of degrees, respective jewels are worn by the various officers, but basically all members wear a special robe of white, having a red border or edging. The presentation of the jewel of the Order is an integral part of the ceremony and it is a small enamelled jewel comprising of two interlaced triangles, in the centre of which is a Lotus Flower, the symbol of the Order; it also features the three emblematic colours of the degrees, which are red, blue and yellow.

THE DEGREES
This society of freemasons supplies a series of grades and

possesses rituals which illustrate the old world religions and notable mythologies of India, with sidelights from the cults of ancient Egypt, Greece and Rome. While this may appear to be a vast subject to encompass in a single order, the material is cast in such a manner as to present a series of ceremonies and lectures which confer instruction on the oriental ideas of Theology and Cosmogony in a most convenient form. A practice which is of special significance to the Order, is the regular observance of the ceremonies of the Vernal and Autumnal Equinoxes. In this Order members endeavour to grasp the inner meaning of masonry and to focus the occult light on items of ritual which might otherwise be without meaning.

Jewel of the Order of Light.

Order of Eri

HISTORY and ORIGIN

This remote and elite Order is said to be derived from a very ancient Order in Ireland, consisting of freemasons and said to have been erected and patronised by the Kings of Ireland, for it is claimed that in early times Erin (Ireland) possessed a literature and history equal to that of the most highly developed of ancient nations. While it is generally accepted that Bro John Yarker (1833–1913) was at one time head of the 'English Revived Order of the Red Branch of Eri', certain records of the Order relate that Bro F. G. Irwin, while Worshipful Master of the Inhabitants Lodge No 178 at Gibraltar in 1858, received the Order at the hands of the captain of an American trading vessel, to whom it had been transmitted from father to son, dating back to 1757, when his Irish forbear emigrated to New York while a District Grand Master of the Order. Major Irwin is then purported to have restored and reorganised the degree in England under the aegis of the Grand Mur-Ollamham. The order possesses two Psalters, the Major Psalter being basically the rituals of the degrees and the Minor Psalter comprising the laws and rules of the order. The degrees embodied in this Order are:

1. Man-at-Arms
2. Esquire
3. Knight

There are three Chapters of the Order; meeting in London and the Midlands as well as in Australia.

STRUCTURE and QUALIFICATION

In this order Chapters are termed Faslairts with an office structure as under:

Enlightened Knight Commander
Treasurer
Secretary
Ollamh
Brehon
Crimtear
Marshall
Bard
Conductor
Captain of Guards
Herald
Assistant Marshal
Sentinel

Admission to this order is strictly by invitation only and is restricted to members of the Societas Rosicruciana in Anglia who have attained the fifth grade or above. The Order is governed by a Most Enlightened Grand Master who is supported by eight Knights Grand Cross and also a retinue of hierarchy designated Ard Officers who constitute the Grand Mur-Ollamham.

REGALIA

The jewel of the order is a gilt metal Celtic cross in red enamel, encircled by a 'rayed' band in green enamel, and is worn on

The jewel of the Order of Eri.

the left breast. An Enlightened Knight Commander wears a Celtic cross and circlet of similar colouring surmounted by a coronet on which are mounted nine Shamrock leaves (five visible), the whole being suspended from a green collarette one inch in width; in the case of Ard Officers the crowned jewel is suspended from a collarette, light blue in colour.

The elite holders of the Grand Cross of Eri wear a gilt collarette of special significance and design, from which is suspended a red enamelled cross having three bars, while an impressive seven-pointed star is worn on the left breast. A sash having five bands of colour is worn tied around the waist.

THE DEGREES

Legend relates that this Order, comprising of freemasons, was founded in 1697 BC by the King of Ireland, finally ceasing its military activities between AD 1649–1659. An ancient book entitled *The Annals of the Four Masters of Ireland* tells of the Knights of the Collar of Eri as instituted by King Eamhium and his eight princes over the armies of the four provinces, ie Ulster, Munster, Leinster and Connaught. The ancient Knightly Order was comprised of Ollamhs who were the teachers and hospitallers, the Brehons who as judges ensured that the laws were correctly administered, the Cruimthears being priests who attended to the religious and moral education of the people, the Bards as historians who preserved the memory of the noble deeds of their ancestors and the later Heralds who assisted in developing the Arts and Sciences.

Much of the modern ceremonies are couched in Bardic Verse and include much ancient Irish lore. The grades are:

Man-at-Arms: The candidate is admitted under an exhortation of a celebrated Celtic Bard by the name of Mac Leag (AD 1015) and in a simple yet impressive ceremony, is duly armed.

Esquire: Reception into the second degree is promulgated through the interpretation of an important charge which stimulates the candidate to demonstrate humility and service in supporting the honourable creed of the ancient kings.

Knight: In this, the last degree, the aspirant is encouraged to engage in figurative combat and his reward is the acclaim of his Brother Knights, to commemorate the mighty deeds of their forbears at the Battle of Ossary. After investiture he is instructed in the Ancient Mysteries and Legends of the Order by the Brehon.

Holy Order of Knights Beneficent of the Holy City

HISTORY and ORIGIN

The Knights Beneficent of the Holy City, more commonly referred to as Chevaliers Bienfaisant de la Cite Sainte (CBCS), took its rise following a Convention held at Wilhelmsbad in 1782 and is the oldest order connected with freemasonry which has had a continuous existence. It is derived from the Rite of Strict Observance erected in 1754, the foundation of which was attributed to Baron von Hund; it propounded a theory that freemasonry was developed directly from the Crusading Templars, embodying a belief that the Order was ruled by 'unknown superiors'. At one time it had many Provinces scattered throughout Europe, but slowly over some 28 years the influence of the Strict Observance waned and it was finally reconstructed to become the Scottish Rectified Rite (CBCS). The degrees of the Order (not fully worked by all Priories) are those practised in the Lodge of St Andrew and The Order of the Interior, operating under the Great Priory of Helvetia. The grades of the Rite are structured as under:

Conferred in a Symbolic Lodge

    1. Entered Apprentice
    2. Fellowcraft
    3. Master Mason

Conferred in a Great Priory

    4. (a) Scottish Master of St Andrew
       (b) Perfect Master of St Andrew

5.　　Squire Novice
6.　　Knight Beneficent of the Holy City

In addition to Switzerland there are today five other Great Priories in the world, situated in the following countries: USA (erected 1934), France (1935), England (1937), Germany (1959) and Belgium (1986). In England the CBCS is controlled by the Great Priory of the United Military, Religious and Masonic Order of the Temple etc, but little is known of its membership as meetings are very infrequent and normally only held when a new member is received.

STRUCTURE and QUALIFICATION

Each Great Priory is governed by a Most Reverend Great Prior, who normally holds the office ad vitam. He is supported by a Deputy Great Prior, a Great Chancellor (Grand Secretary) and three Prefects, while members are referred to as Reverend Knights. Membership is strictly limited and the prerogative of invitation lies firmly in the hands of the hierarchy, so much so, that the Order is seldom if ever referred to in masonic circles (except possibly among CBCS members) and qualification is restricted to only the most senior members of Great Priory of the Temple.

REGALIA

The Grades of St Andrew: The regalia in the first two grades of the Order consists of a reversible collarette of red on the one side and thistle green on the other. To this is attached a bronze pierced medallion featuring a circular wreath of laurel leaves in the centre of which are two 'rayed' interlaced triangles and upon these is superimposed a figure of the crucified St Andrew, this being surmounted by an imperial crown. The reverse of the jewel also features the interlaced triangle pattern and this is charged with the letter H having a square and compasses above and below respectively, and framed by a level and a plumb rule.

The collarette jewel of Squire and Knight Beneficent of the Holy Order of Knights Beneficent of the Holy City.

Squire and Knight Beneficent: The regalia of these grades comprises of a red collarette edged with gold braid from which is suspended a superb jewelled cross of the Order, it normally being of pure gold with four segmental arms and a centre segment, all in ruby or similar coloured stone. On the reverse of this cross are engraved the initials of the secret motto of the Priory, together with a Roman numeral denoting the number of the province. The bronze jewel of the first two grades is now worn attached to the point of a four-inch wide sash of white watered silk, which is worn over the right shoulder and bears a red embroidered 'rayed' cross of similar dimensions to that on the collarette, also bearing the initials and Roman numeral together with a rosette at the point of the sash which has a red button in the centre.

THE DEGREES

The two degrees of St Andrew which are conferred in a Chapter were presumably split from an original single degree of that name, but have no connection whatever with Scotland.

Scottish Master of St Andrew: This grade makes reference to the divine tradition of the Temple of Solomon and the abiding presence of the Holy Shekinah. It also infers that while the first Temple was laid to ruins there still remained within the sacred knowledge of the God of Israel.

Perfect Master of St Andrew: Here the legend of the second Temple is developed, exhorting the true seeker to penetrate the tomb of Hiram in search of the lost word. His labours are rewarded by the allegorical personality of the Master Builder being raised like a veil to reveal the risen Christ and thereby unfolds a Christian interpretation of the letters forming the name of our GM; it also hints at the coming of the New Jerusalem, the mystic Zion.

Squire Novice: This grade, like that of a Knight, is conferred in a Commandery and recounts a legend that at the dawn of the Christian era, wise and illuminated sages dwelling within the Holy City were converted to Christianity by St Mark. The secret work of initiation required that their doctrine be transmitted by secret oral tradition, which was done and culminated in the Knights Templar who were reputed to be the latter custodians of this divine knowledge.

Knight Benĕficent of the Holy City: In the final grade it is revealed to the Novice that at the zenith of ancient Egyptian civilisation and even with Orpheus, Pythagoras and Pluto a religious dogma existed, which was identical with that of Christianity. It is further explained that the Chivalry of the Holy City was manifested in good works being the perfect path to God and by the diffusion of such works ensuring the greatest good to the human family and the final attainment of the true enlightenment.

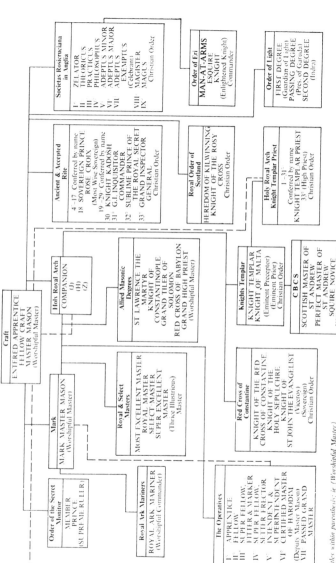

Craft	Holy Royal Arch	Ancient & Accepted Rite	Societas Rosicruciana in Anglia

Craft

ENTERED APPRENTICE
FELLOW CRAFT
MASTER MASON
(Worshipful Master)

Holy Royal Arch

COMPANION
(J)
(H)
(Z)

Ancient & Accepted Rite

4–17	Conferred by name
18	SOVEREIGN PRINCE ROSE CROIX (Most Wise Sovereign)
19–29	Conferred by name
30	KNIGHT KADOSH
31	G. INQUISITOR COMMANDER
32	SUBLIME PRINCE OF THE ROYAL SECRET
33	GRAND INSPECTOR GENERAL

Christian Order

Societas Rosicruciana in Anglia

I	ZELATOR
II	THEORICUS
III	PRACTICUS
IV	PHILOSOPHUS
V	ADEPTUS MINOR
VI	ADEPTUS MAJOR
VII	ADEPTUS EXEMPTUS
VIII	MAGISTER (Celebrant)
IX	MAGUS

Christian Order

Royal Order of Scotland

HEREDOM OF KILWINNING
KNIGHT OF THE ROSY CROSS
Christian Order

MAN-AT-ARMS

ESQUIRE
KNIGHT
(Enlightened Knight)
COMMANDER

Order of Eri

Order of Light

FIRST DEGREE
(Guardian of Light)
PASSING DEGREE
(Pres. of Garuda)
SECOND DEGREE
(Indra)

Holy Royal Arch Knight Templar Priest

1–31	Conferred by name
	KNIGHT TEMPLAR PRIEST
33	(High Priest)

Christian Order

Allied Masonic Degrees

ST LAWRENCE THE MARTYR
KNIGHT OF CONSTANTINOPLE
GRAND TILER OF SOLOMON
RED CROSS OF BABYLON
GRAND HIGH PRIEST
(Worshipful Master)

Knights Templar

KNIGHT TEMPLAR
KNIGHT OF MALTA
(Eminent Preceptor)
(Eminent Prior)
Christian Order

C B C S

SCOTTISH MASTER OF ST ANDREW
PERFECT MASTER OF ST ANDREW
SQUIRE NOVICE
KNIGHT BENEFICENT
Christian Order

Mark

MARK MASTER MASON
(Worshipful Master)

Royal & Select Masters

MOST EXCELLENT MASTER
ROYAL MASTER
SELECT MASTER
SUPER EXCELLENT MASTER
(Three Illustrious) Master

Red Cross of Constantine

KNIGHT OF THE RED CROSS OF CONSTANTINE
KNIGHT OF THE HOLY SEPULCHRE
KNIGHT OF ST JOHN THE EVANGELIST
(Viceroy)
(Sovereign)
Christian Order

Order of the Secret Monitor

MEMBER
PRINCE
(SUPREME RULER)

Royal Ark Mariners

ROYAL ARK MARINER
(Worshipful Commander)

The Operatives

I	APPRENTICE
II	FELLOW
III	SUPER FELLOW, FITTER & MARKER
IV	SUPER FELLOW, SETTER ERECTOR
V	INTENDENT & SUPERINTENDENT
VI	CERTIFIED MASTER or HARODIM (Deputy Master Mason)
VII	PASSED GRAND MASTER

Titles within parenthesis; ie (Worshipful Master) indicates the deocration and chronological position of the Chair.

DEGREE COMPARISON CHART

ENGLAND	DEGREE	USA	SCOTLAND	IRELAND
—	PAST MASTER MASON	General Grand Chapter of Royal Arch Masons	—	—
Bristol Chapters only	EXCELLENT MASTER	Gd Council AMD		
Supreme Grand Chapter	ROYAL ARCH MASON	General Grand Chapter of Royal Arch Masons	Supreme Grand Chapter of Royal Arch Masons and Grand Lodge	Supreme Grand Royal Arch Chapter
Grand Lodge of Mark Master Masons	MARK MASTER MASON			
	ROYAL ARK MARINER	Grand Council of Allied Masonic Degrees		—
Grand Council of the Order of the Secret Monitor	MEMBER	—	—	—
	PRINCE	—	—	—
	SUPREME RULER	—	—	—
Grand Council of Royal & Select Masters	MOST EXCELLENT MASTER	—	—	—
	ROYAL MASTER	General Grand Council of Royal & Select Masters	Supreme Grand Chapter of Royal Arch Masons	—
	SELECT MASTER			—
	SUPER EXCELLENT MASTER			—
Grand Council of Allied Masonic Degrees	ST LAWRENCE THE MARTYR	Grand Council of Allied Masonic Degrees	—	—
	KNIGHT OF CONSTANTINOPLE		—	—
	GRAND TILER OF SOLOMON			—
	RED CROSS OF BABYLON	Grand Encampment of Knights Templar	Red Cross Knight on Babylonish Pass	—
	GRAND HIGH PRIEST	General Grand Chapter of Royal Arch Masons	—	—

ENGLAND	DEGREE	USA	SCOTLAND	IRELAND
— — — —	SECRET MONITOR / ARCHITECT / GRAND ARCHITECT / SUPERINTENDANT / MASTER OF TYRE	Grand Council of Allied Masonic Degrees	— — — —	— — — —
Supreme Council for England & Wales	ANCIENT & ACCEPTED RITE 4°–33°	Supreme Councils for USA (Northern & Southern Jurisdictions)	Supreme Council for Scotland	Supreme Council for Ireland
Grand Imperial Conclave of the Red Cross of Constantine of England and Wales etc.	RED CROSS OF CONSTANTINE / KNIGHT OF THE HOLY SEPULCHRE / KNIGHT OF ST JOHN THE EVANGELIST	Grand Imperial Conclave of the Red Cross of Constantine (various State Councils)	Grand Imperial Conclave of the Red Cross of Constantine of Scotland	—
— —	KNIGHT OF THE SWORD / KNIGHT OF THE EAST / KNIGHT OF THE EAST & WEST	Knight Masons of the USA	see Red Cross of Babylon	Knight Masons of Ireland
Great Priory of the Temple & Malta of England & Wales etc.	KNIGHT TEMPLAR / KNIGHT OF MALTA	Grand Encampment of Knights Templar of the USA	Great Priory of the Temple & Malta of Scotland	Great Priory of the Temple of Ireland —
Grand College of HRAKTP of England	HOLY ROYAL ARCH KNIGHT TEMPLAR PRIEST	Grand College of HRAKTP of the USA	—	—
Provinces of the Royal Order of Scotland	HEREDOM OF KILWINNING / KNIGHT OF THE ROSY CROSS	Province of the Royal Order of Scotland	Grand Lodge Royal Order of Scotland (Edinburgh) also Provinces	—

ENGLAND	DEGREE		USA	SCOTLAND	IRELAND
Worshipful Society of Free Masons etc.	I°	APPRENTICE	—	—	—
	II°	FELLOW	—	—	—
	III°	FITTER & MARKER	—	—	—
	IV°	SETTER & ERECTOR	—	—	—
	V°	INTENDENT etc	—	—	—
	VI°	CERTIFIED MASTER	—	—	—
	VII°	PASSED GRAND MASTER			—
					—
Societas Rosicruciana in Anglia	I°	ZELATOR	Societas Rosicruciana in Civitatibus Foederatis	Societas Rosicruciana in Scotia	—
	II°	THEORICUS			—
	III°	PRACTICUS			—
	IV°	PHILOSOPHUS			—
	V°	ADEPTUS MINOR			—
	VI°	ADEPTUS MAJOR			
	VII°	ADEPTUS EXEMPTUS			
	VIII°	MAGISTER			
	IX°	MAGUS			
					—
August Order of Light		FIRST DEGREE	—	—	—
		PASSING DEGREE	—	—	
		SECOND DEGREE	—		
					—
Order of Eri		MAN-AT-ARMS	Grand Council of Allied Masonic Degrees	—	—
		ESQUIRE		—	
		KNIGHT OF ERI		—	—
Great Priory of England of Knights Beneficent of the Holy City		SCOTTISH MASTER OF ST ANDREW	Great Priory of the USA of Knights Beneficent of the Holy City	—	
		PERFECT MASTER OF ST ANDREW		—	—
		SQUIRE NOVICE			
		KNIGHT BENEFICENT OF THE HOLY CITY		—	—

The SQUARE

The Independent Magazine for Freemasons Everywhere

Published quarterly in March, June, September and December *The Square* is for every freemason whatever rank, with articles of a general nature on all manner of masonic topics: news, views, overseas, book reviews, guidance, history and much more.

64pp inc colour £2.50

For subscription details
please contact:
THE SQUARE
Ian Allan Publishing Ltd
Riverdene Business Park
Molesey Road
Hersham
Surrey KT12 4RG

Tel: 01932 266600
Fax: 01932 266601

Lewis Masonic

MASONIC HANDBOOK
SERIES FROM

Lewis Masonic

This popular series of masonic handbooks gives the reader a thorough introduction and comprehensive guidance to the duties of each office. These handbooks are not rituals. Avoid pitfalls and learn how to perform the duties efficiently and expertly.

A HANDBOOK FOR THE WORSHIPFUL MASTER

Revised edition
F. Rich 160pp
210mm x 148mm h/c
£12.95 (ref: 0095)

THE DIRECTOR OF CEREMONIES

C. Carter 104pp
210mm x 148mm h/c
£7.95 (ref: 0039)

THE DIRECTOR OF CEREMONIES
(Pocket Edition)

32pp 76mm x 50mm
s/c £2.50 (ref: 0056)

THE LODGE ALMONER

Revised edition
C. Carter 88pp
210mm x 148mm h/c
£10.95 (ref: 0029)

THE PRECEPTOR'S HANDBOOK

C. Carter 96pp 210mm
x 148mm h/c £10.95
(ref: 0062)

THE INNER GUARD AND DEACONS

C. Carter 96pp
210mm x 148mm h/c
£7.95 (ref: 0027)

A GUIDE TO THE TYLER'S WORK

D. Adams 56pp
210mm x 148mm s/c
£5.95 (ref: 0079)

MISCELLANY OF ALTERNATIVE WORKINGS

80pp 210mm x 148mm
s/c £3.00 (ref: 0086)

THE MASONIC TREASURER

A. Nelson 128pp
210mm x 148mm h/c
£7.95 (ref: 0054)

A GUIDE FOR THE MASTERS ELECT

N. Halliday 64pp
210mm x 148mm s/c
£6.00 (ref: 0057)

THE LODGE SECRETARY

C. Carter 134pp
210mm x 148mm h/c
£11.00 (ref: 0015)

NEW

THE WARDENS, CHAPLAIN, IPM & PAST MASTERS

C. Carter
210mm x 148mm h/c
£12.95 (ref: 0021)

**Available from: Lewis Masonic, 4 Watling Drive, Hinckley, Leics LE10 3EY
Tel: 01455 233747 Enquiries: 01932 266600**